First World War
and Army of Occupation
War Diary
France, Belgium and Germany

61 DIVISION
182 Infantry Brigade,
Brigade Machine Gun Company
16 June 1916 - 28 February 1918

WO95/3057/3

The Naval & Military Press Ltd
www.nmarchive.com
Published in association with The National Archives

Published by

The Naval & Military Press Ltd

Unit 10 Ridgewood Industrial Park,

Uckfield, East Sussex,

TN22 5QE England

Tel: +44 (0) 1825 749494

www.naval-military-press.com

www.nmarchive.com

This diary has been reprinted in facsimile from the original. Any imperfections are inevitably reproduced and the quality may fall short of modern type and cartographic standards.

© Crown Copyright
Images reproduced by permission of The National Archives, London, England, 2015.

Contents

Document type	Place/Title	Date From	Date To
Heading	WO95/3057/3 182 Brigade Machine Gun Company		
Heading	182nd Machine Gun Coy Jun 1916 Feb 1918		
War Diary	Grantham	16/06/1916	16/06/1916
War Diary	Southampton	16/06/1916	16/06/1916
War Diary	Le Harvre	17/06/1916	18/06/1916
War Diary	La Gorgue	19/06/1916	19/06/1916
War Diary	Lestrem	19/06/1916	23/06/1916
War Diary	Le Drumez	23/06/1916	31/07/1916
Heading	War Diary Of 182nd Machine Gun Company August 1916 Vol 3		
War Diary	Le Drumez (M.3.c.3.2)	01/08/1916	31/08/1916
Heading	War Diary of 182nd Machine Gun Coy From 1.9.16 to 30.9.16 (Volume)		
War Diary	Lestrem	01/09/1916	02/09/1916
War Diary	Laventie	03/09/1916	28/10/1916
War Diary	Estaires	29/10/1916	29/10/1916
War Diary	Merville	30/10/1916	31/10/1916
Heading	War Diary of 182nd Machine Gun Company From Nov 1st 1916 to Nov 30th 1916		
War Diary	Merville	01/11/1916	02/11/1916
War Diary	Gonnehem	03/11/1916	03/11/1916
War Diary	Auchel	04/11/1916	04/11/1916
War Diary	Ostreville	05/11/1916	05/11/1916
War Diary	Cannettemont	06/11/1916	06/11/1916
War Diary	Beauvoir	07/11/1916	15/11/1916
War Diary	Berneuil	16/11/1916	16/11/1916
War Diary	Berteaucourt	17/11/1916	17/11/1916
War Diary	Rubempre	18/11/1916	18/11/1916
War Diary	Warloy	19/11/1916	21/11/1916
War Diary	Albert	22/11/1916	22/11/1916
War Diary	Senlis	23/11/1916	27/11/1916
War Diary	Hedauville	28/11/1916	30/11/1916
Heading	No 182 Machine Gun Company War Diary December 1st 1916 To December 31st 1916 (Volume 7)		
War Diary	Hedauville	01/12/1916	02/12/1916
War Diary	Martinsart	03/12/1916	10/12/1916
War Diary	Mouquet Farm	11/12/1916	20/12/1916
War Diary	Martinsart	20/12/1916	22/12/1916
War Diary	Hedauville	23/12/1916	30/12/1916
War Diary	Martinsart	31/12/1916	31/12/1916
Heading	182nd Machine Gun Company War Diary For January 1917 Volume VIII		
War Diary	Martinsart	01/01/1917	06/01/1917
War Diary	Mouquet Farm	07/01/1917	15/01/1917
War Diary	Rubempre	16/01/1917	17/01/1917
War Diary	Gorges	18/01/1917	18/01/1917
War Diary	Cramont	19/01/1917	19/01/1917
War Diary	Forest L'Abbaye	20/01/1917	31/01/1917
Heading	182 M.G.C War Diary February 1917 Volume No IX		
War Diary	Forest L'Abbaye	01/02/1917	05/02/1917

Type	Location	From	To
War Diary	St Firmin	06/02/1917	10/02/1917
War Diary	Hautvillers	11/02/1917	11/02/1917
War Diary	Bellancourt	12/02/1917	15/02/1917
War Diary	Auber Court	16/02/1917	19/02/1917
War Diary	Vauvillers	20/02/1917	25/02/1917
War Diary	Vermandovillers	25/02/1917	28/02/1917
Heading	182 Machine Gun Coy War Diary For March 1917 Volume X		
War Diary	Vermandovillers	01/03/1917	08/03/1917
War Diary	Harbonnieres	09/03/1917	14/03/1917
War Diary	Deniecourt	15/03/1917	17/03/1917
War Diary	Ablain Court	17/03/1917	18/03/1917
War Diary	Marchele Pot	19/03/1917	25/03/1917
War Diary	Pargny	26/03/1917	26/03/1917
War Diary	Devise	27/03/1917	27/03/1917
War Diary	Tertry	28/03/1917	29/03/1917
War Diary	Devise	30/03/1917	31/03/1917
Heading	No 182 M G Coy War Diary 1st April 1917 To 30th April 1917 (Volume 11)		
War Diary	Devise	01/04/1917	01/04/1917
War Diary	Meraucourt	02/04/1917	06/04/1917
War Diary	Villeveque	07/04/1917	12/04/1917
War Diary	Quivieres	13/04/1917	20/04/1917
War Diary	Savy	20/04/1917	30/04/1917
Heading	No 182 Machine Gun Company War Diary From 1st May 1917 To 31st May 1917 Volume-12		
War Diary	Savy	01/05/1917	14/05/1917
War Diary	Germaine & Curchy	15/05/1917	16/05/1917
War Diary	Olincourt Chateau Flesselles	17/05/1917	17/05/1917
War Diary	Olincourt	18/05/1917	20/05/1917
War Diary	Longuevillette	21/05/1917	22/05/1917
War Diary	Ivergny	23/05/1917	24/05/1917
War Diary	Berneville	25/05/1917	31/05/1917
Heading	No 182 Machine Gun Coy War Diary June 1st 1917 To June 30th 1917 (Volume13)		
War Diary	Arras	01/06/1917	11/06/1917
War Diary	Dainville	12/06/1917	22/06/1917
War Diary	Wail	23/06/1917	30/06/1917
Heading	War Diary Of No 182 Machine Gun Coy July 1st To July 31st (Volume 14)		
War Diary	Wail	01/07/1917	23/07/1917
War Diary	Sibbeville	24/07/1917	24/07/1917
War Diary	Rubrouck Area	25/07/1917	31/07/1917
Heading	War Diary No. 182 Machine Gun Coy From 1st Aug 1917 To 31st Aug 1917 (Volume 15)		
War Diary	Rubrouck	01/08/1917	15/08/1917
War Diary	Brandhoek No 1 Area	16/08/1917	21/08/1917
War Diary	Frezenberg (23.c.4.7)	22/08/1917	22/08/1917
War Diary	Brandhoek 1	23/08/1917	23/08/1917
War Diary	Wieltje Sector	24/08/1917	29/08/1917
War Diary	Brandhoek No 1	30/08/1917	31/08/1917
Heading	War Diary No. 182 Machine Gun Coy From 1st Sept 1917 To 30th Sept 1917 (Volume 16)		
War Diary	Rubrouck No.1	01/09/1917	03/09/1917
War Diary	Wieltje Sector	04/09/1917	12/09/1917
War Diary	Brandhoek	13/09/1917	14/09/1917

War Diary	Sehoudenhoek	15/09/1917	17/09/1917
War Diary	Eecke Area	17/09/1917	19/09/1917
War Diary	Berneville	20/09/1917	22/09/1917
War Diary	St. Nicholas Area	23/09/1917	24/09/1917
War Diary	Fampoux	25/09/1917	30/09/1917
Heading	War Diary No. 182 Machine Gun Coy From 1st October 1917 To 31st October 1917 (Volume-17)		
War Diary	Fampoux	01/10/1917	16/10/1917
War Diary	Arras	16/10/1917	26/10/1917
War Diary	Greenland Hill Sector	27/10/1917	31/10/1917
Heading	182 Machine Gun Company War Diary From 1st November 1917 To 31st November 1917 (Volume 18)		
War Diary	Greenland Hill Sector	01/11/1917	21/11/1917
War Diary	Arras	22/11/1917	28/11/1917
War Diary	Dainville	29/11/1917	30/11/1917
War Diary	Beaume	30/11/1917	30/11/1917
War Diary	Trescault	30/11/1917	30/11/1917
Heading	No 182 Machine Gun Coy War Diary From 1st December 1917 To 31st December 1917 (Volume XIX)		
War Diary	Havrin Court Wood	01/12/1917	01/12/1917
War Diary	Gouzeaucourt Wood	02/12/1917	02/12/1917
War Diary	N Of La Vacquerie	03/12/1917	06/12/1917
War Diary	Havrin Court Wood	07/12/1917	09/12/1917
War Diary	W. Of La Vacquerie	10/12/1917	16/12/1917
War Diary	Havrin Court Wood	17/12/1918	18/12/1918
War Diary	Manan Court	19/12/1917	23/12/1917
War Diary	Sailly-Le-Sec	24/12/1917	29/12/1917
War Diary	Aubercourt	30/12/1917	31/12/1917
War Diary	Fresnoy-En-Chaussee	01/01/1918	06/01/1918
War Diary	Billancourt	07/01/1918	08/01/1918
War Diary	Savy	09/01/1918	10/01/1918
War Diary	S.10.c.30.95 Ref S 62b Siv 1.20000	11/01/1918	18/01/1918
War Diary	Vaux	19/01/1918	26/01/1918
War Diary	Fresnoy Le Petit	27/01/1918	31/01/1918
Heading	War Diary No 182 Machine Gun Company From February 1st To February 28th (Volume 21)		
War Diary	Fresnoy Le Petit	01/02/1918	11/02/1918
War Diary	Vaux	12/02/1918	19/02/1918
War Diary	S10.c.35.9	20/02/1918	28/02/1918

WO 95/3057/3

182 Brigade Machine Gun Company.

61ST DIVISION
182ND INFY BDE

182ND MACHINE GUN COY.
JUN 1916-FEB 1918.

WAR DIARY or INTELLIGENCE SUMMARY

Army Form C. 2118.

182 M/G Coy

(Erase heading not required.)

Instructions regarding War Diaries and Intelligence Summaries are contained in F.S. Regs., Part II and the Staff Manual respectively. Title Pages will be prepared in manuscript.

Place	Date	Hour	Summary of Events and Information	Remarks and references to Appendices
Grantham	16.6.16	6.30 am	182 M.G. Coy left for Southampton	N.O
Southampton	16.6.16	9.15 pm	Left Southampton S.S. "Caesarea"	nil
Le Havre	17.6.16	3.45 am	Arrived. Proceeded to No.1 Base Camp	nil
do	18.6.16	7.35 pm	Left Le Havre for La Gorgue	N.O
La Gorgue	19.6.16	9.10 pm	Arrived La Gorgue. Proceeded to Lestrem where we billeted.	N.O
LESTREM	20.6.16			N.O
do	21.6.16	10.0 am	Inspection by Divisional General 182nd Brigade in trenches.	N.O
do	22.6.16	11.55 pm	Received orders to move following day to LE DRUMEZ.	N.O
do	23.6.16	11.30 am	Left LA GORGUE for LE DRUMEZ.	N.O
LE DRUMEZ	do	1.30 pm	Arrived at LE DRUMEZ and went into billets. We are attached for instruction to No.104 M.G. Coy (Major PARKER). Brought fighting limbers and G.S. Wagon only.	N.O
do	do	6.30 pm	Transport, excluding 8 limbers, returning to LESTREM.	N.O
do	do	do	2½ Sections (A, B + ½ C) went into trenches (without guns) for instruction.	N.O
do	24.6.16	9.5 am	Went round trenches with Major Parker. (5 guns in front line - 5 in support + 6 in reserve at Company H.Q. at LE DRUMEZ.)	N.O

WAR DIARY
or
INTELLIGENCE SUMMARY
(Erase heading not required.)

Army Form C. 2118.

Instructions regarding War Diaries and Intelligence Summaries are contained in F. S. Regs., Part II. and the Staff Manual respectively. Title Pages will be prepared in manuscript.

182/15 (M)

Place	Date	Hour	Summary of Events and Information	Remarks and references to Appendices
LE DRUMEZ	25.6.16	11.15 pm	64 guns (M.G.) opened fire on German communication trenches & roads at back of their line.	Nil
do	do	11.45 pm	Backguns fired right. Another belt for gun fired.	Nil
			Germans seemed nervous at first bombardment and sent up many Verey lights; they did not take much notice of second bombardment however.	
do	26.6.16		Enemy artillery fairly active in afternoon.	Nil
do	do	11.45 -12.45	Very heavy bombardment of German trenches which they replied to with great vigour. No casualties amongst our gunners. At midnight we took over trenches from 101 M.G. Coy.	Nil
			To whom we were transfered & attached.	
do	27.6.16		All quiet. Our guns kept open gaps in enemy wire; they reported disturbing an enemy party but it was unsatisfactory.	Nil
do	28.6.16		Nothing to report. Guns kept open gaps in enemy wire during night. Four reserve guns fired indirect fire at enemy communication trenches & light railways N25C 3&4, N25 A73 (in front lines) The enemy did not make any reply.	Nil
do	29.6.16		Quiet during day. All guns ordered to fire at enemy parapet at following times:- 2.30 am, 3.5 am, 3.45 am & 4.20 am to cover attack on our right.	Nil
do	30.6.16	30 pm	Took over right of line from No 183 M.G. Coy (Capt WALKER.) Headquarters still at LE DRUMEZ M3C 32. Company now holds whole of 182nd Brigade front - 8 guns in front line and 8 in support. Line is a long one.	Nil

Army Form C. 2118/

Vol XI 2

WAR DIARY
or
INTELLIGENCE SUMMARY
(Erase heading not required.)

Instructions regarding War Diaries and Intelligence Summaries are contained in F.S. Regs., Part II. and the Staff Manual respectively. Title Pages will be prepared in manuscript.

182nd Machine Gun Company

Place	Date	Hour	Summary of Events and Information	Remarks and references to Appendices
LE BRUNEZ	1.7.16		All quiet during day	NIL
do	do	9.30 pm	Enemy bombarded whole Brigade Front heavily, inflicting severe damage between M30c1535 & M35b7537. Trenches badly damaged and machine gun defences destroyed. Machine gun sent from support to cover gap.	NIL
do	2.7.16		Quiet. Trenches being rebuilt. Some still enemy guns.	NIL
do	3.7.16	3.0 pm	No 3 Section relieves No 2. Return in front line to Nonneboom. Brigade complimented by Corps Commander for splendid machine gun fire.	NIL
			All quiet.	
do	4.7.16		Quiet during day.	NIL
		10.40	Our artillery bombarded "BIRDCAGE" heavily. Machine guns fired infilade if "BIRDCAGE". Enemy's reply not very effective, but one M.G. in No 11 Emplacement hit & knocked out. Gun very hot so replaced it.	NIL
			Barrel casing punctured by shrapnel. Gun very hot so replaced it by new one in support.	NIL
		11.5	Artillery lifted to form barrage at back of BIRDCAGE	NIL
		11.45	Artillery ceased fire. Idea being to deceive enemy & make him believe that raid on "BIRDCAGE" was intended. Attack takes place on our left by 183 Bde.	NIL
do	5.7.16		Quiet during day. Order to fire until 3.0 am kept. Company. Order & hour of return unaltered.	NIL

2449 Wt. W14957/M90 750,000 1/16 J.B.C. & A. Forms/C.2118/12.

Army Form C. 2118.

WAR DIARY
or
INTELLIGENCE SUMMARY
(Erase heading not required.)

Instructions regarding War Diaries and Intelligence Summaries are contained in F.S. Regs., Part II. and the Staff Manual respectively. Title Pages will be prepared in manuscript.

Place	Date	Hour	Summary of Events and Information	Remarks and references to Appendices
LE DRUMEZ	6.7.16		as usual in regard to sending off flares in wrong directions it is necessary to fire very lights for every gun.	137th MG Coy
do	7.7.16		Quiet during day. Guns fired at usual gaps in enemy wire by night & gun from outpost line employed indirect fire.	hid
do	8.7.16		Quiet during day. Went to MERVILLE with D.A.D.O.S. to Heavy Mobile Workshop and inspected a new mounting (CLARK & JARVIS Patent). The mounting seems excellent & we are to give it a trial. It will be of great service for indirect fire. They informed us at MERVILLE that within a day of its being used, a gun mounted on one of these mountings had three German batteries searching for it.	hid
		11.0 pm	Right & left flank guns enfiladed German line. Our guns firing from M.24.c.4.1. and M.5.B.10.13. onwards. Complaint that some of our shots hit our own parapets. Bowret in good condition. Legs of tripod sandbagged and sandbags under trail casing. Have seen to faulty ammunition.	hid
do	9.7.16		Quiet during day. Usual artillery practice in afternoon. Fire from our artillery seemed very accurate. Raid on enemy trenches to be executed at night. Troops (1 Coy 2/5 WARWICKS) to enter trenches at M36.c.o.5. fired very lights. Do as much damage as possible.	hid

WAR DIARY
or
INTELLIGENCE SUMMARY
(Erase heading not required.)

Army Form C. 2118.

192nd M.C. Coy

Place	Date	Hour	Summary of Events and Information	Remarks and references to Appendices
Le BRUMEZ	9.7.16 (cont d)		Two of our guns to form barrage North of track of point of entry. Guns placed at following points N13 b & b6, and M35 d 4.5 to fire to M36 c 33 and M36 d 5.1 respectively. Guns have orders not to traverse to right or left but remain between the points given showing two barrages almost parallel.	M.D.
do	10.7.16	11.15 am 11.23 am 12.25 am	Coy (M.G.) given fire to form barrage A.G. to advance of infantry. B.G.C. contact on mine A.G. BRIDGES messing freely. Guns cease fire.	M.D. M.D. M.D.
			Orders received to one M.G. to ceaseful during to form barrage. German's bombard LAVENTIE heavily for about 2½ hours beginning about 6.0 a.m. Quiet during day. Enemy bombard fire on enemy's outpost line during remainder of day.	M.D.
do	11.7.16		At night — nothing to report	M.D.
do	12.7.16		Do	M.D.
do	13.7.16		Quiet during day. Indirect fire M30 d 8½ 6 to N25 c 6 2½ at Railway and dump. Short enemy bombardment with rifle grenades 12.45 pm to 1.15 pm. Heavy bombardment on right of Brigade reputed about midnight. Fired at enemy wire gaps.	M.D.
do	14.7.16		Quiet during day. Orders out for smoke + gas attack but cancelled at 13.15 owing to Received orders to be ready to hand over to 92nd and 93rd M.G. Coys by 12.30 am 15th.	M.D.
do	15.7.16	8.30	Received Orders to meet Capt DUNNE O.C. 92 A. Aus M.G. Coy at ROUGE CROIX at 10 am	M.D.

WAR DIARY
or
INTELLIGENCE SUMMARY

Army Form C. 2118.

182nd M.G. Coy

Place	Date	Hour	Summary of Events and Information	Remarks and references to Appendices
LE DRUMEZ	15/7/16	10:30am	to give us a 4th Coy a march at ROUGE CROIX in charge of Lt Blanc and Lt ROUGE CROIX. Due to SURPRISE gun to give POSTLAME same to MAZEN REDOUBT.	
		8.0 p.m	Mr A BRICKFIELDS (wh. had be noted at (11.10pm) and the 2nd Div. to Le Fleury for and emplacements — 21 — 30 — 10 — 9. Our new heavy guns were resumed by 12th Div M.G Coy of MANCHESTER POST MORTEM GRAFTON, OMCHE HOUSE and No 11 — 25 — 32 in front line. Six of our guns ordered to relieve No 183 M.G Coy in FAUQUISSART SECTOR. Remainder returned to LE DRUMEZ.	
do	16/7/16	11:0am	Service at Hqrs by Capt BENNETT. Received orders to move 12 guns into FAUQUISSART SECTOR to support an attack in 4 numbered and numbered houses next of the RIVIERE des LAYES between the FAUQUISSART — TIRVELET ROAD (exclusive) to dutch summary S.E. Two new trenches past NEUWE SALIENT. One section to each attacking Battalion and in support and one in reserve. Subsection No3 Lieut BAILY to 5 Coy 3rd Warwicks. } Subsection No 2 Mr NUTTING to C Coy 8rd Warwicks. } ATTACKING Subsection No 1 2nd Lt TYACKE A B Coy 1/4 Warwicks. } Subsection No K & CAMPBELL & N Coy 1/4 Warwicks. No 3 Section in support. No 1 Section in reserve at battle headquarters at MASSELOT POST.	

Army Form C. 2118.

WAR DIARY
or
INTELLIGENCE SUMMARY
(Erase heading not required.)

Instructions regarding War Diaries and Intelligence Summaries are contained in F. S. Regs., Part II. and the Staff Manual respectively. Title Pages will be prepared in manuscript.

182nd M.G. Coy

Place	Date	Hour	Summary of Events and Information	Remarks and references to Appendices
			Sections in attack are given orders to support haref with four runs and consolidate former line.	A.O
			Support section to conform to forward suppts until no further plans were telephone had from Coy. Appr. at MASSELOT POST is OFF TURNED in support.	A.O
			Three sections (Battery of support) in Coy. Line were instructed accordingly informed by General that Nick had been progressed owing to bad weather.	A.O
LE DRUMEZ	17/7/16	8.30pm	Received orders to withdraw 2 sections to LEDRUMEZ	A.O
do	18/7/16	2.00am	Two sections arrived at LE DRUMEZ.	A.O
			Nos 1 & 4 sections left me line – 2 guns of No. 3 section on front line to hold from J to K in rear guns of No. 2 section of C Ry H house & FROQUISSART respectively.	
			No 4 section 2 guns at MASSELOT POST	
			1 gun ROAD BEND	
			2 guns MASSELOT HOUSE.	
			Orders received from Bde that attack would take place on 19 inst	A.O
		4.0pm	All guns leave LE DRUMEZ and proceed to FROQUISSART Sector. II, III, IV sections will front line and No I section in reserve at MASSELOT POST.	A.O
do	19/7/16		Dispositions of Company as shown above.	A.O

2449 Wt. W14957/M90 750,000 1/16 J.B.C. & A. Forms/C.2118/12.

Army Form C. 2118.

WAR DIARY
or
INTELLIGENCE SUMMARY
(Erase heading not required.)

Instructions regarding War Diaries and Intelligence Summaries are contained in F. S. Regs., Part II. and the Staff Manual respectively. Title Pages will be prepared in manuscript.

Place	Date	Hour	Summary of Events and Information	Remarks and references to Appendices
LE DRUMEZ	19.7.16		No II Section in front line to attack with 2/7 Warwicks (on right)	182nd M.G. Coy
			No IV " " " " " " " " (on left) } with 1st wave of attack
			No III Section in front line in support (in centre)
			No I Section at MASSELOT POST, which was also Company H.Q. and connected by telephone with our photo.
			Zero time 11.0 a.m.
			Time Table. 2.00 to 2.30 Registration by Artillery
			2.30 – 3.00 Bombardment by Heavy Artillery
			3.00 – 4.00 Wirecutting by Artillery
			4.00 – 4.25 do do Naval howitzers
			4.25 – 4.29 Artillery lift
			4.29 – 5.04 Wirecutting
			5.04 – 5.09 Artillery lift
			5.09 – 6.29 Wirecutting and bombardment
			6.29 – 5.30 Artillery lift
			5.30 – 6.21 Wirecutting and bombardment
			6.21 – 6.31 Artillery lift
			6.31 – 7.00 Wirecutting and bombardment
			7.00 Artillery lift and Infantry Assault
			The German trenches were severely dealt with by our artillery and especially by heavy aerial torpedoes, and the wire was well cut.
			By 6.0 p.m. the 2/7 Warwicks had reached the first German line. No II Section going forward with them.

2449 Wt. W14957/M90 750,000 1/16 J.B.C. & A. Forms/C.2118/12.

WAR DIARY
or
INTELLIGENCE SUMMARY
(Erase heading not required.)

Army Form C. 2118.

Instructions regarding War Diaries and Intelligence Summaries are contained in F.S. Regs., Part II. and the Staff Manual respectively. Title Pages will be prepared in manuscript.

Place	Date	Hour	Summary of Events and Information	Remarks and references to Appendices
				182nd M.G. Coy

Only two unwounded men of No II Section returned and they reported that two gun crews (at least) came into action in the enemy front line, one firing across at enemy support coming up from support line and the other firing at enemy bombers (?) that however were all bombed and more succeeded in reaching our lines, both officers of the section were hit — one at and above (?) parapet and the other down to hospital 19th/20th. Each gunner carried 2 Mills grenades and these were the bombs that enabled the remaining few there spare to keep the machine guns to shoot with enemy bombers. On reaching No III section I found the 2/6th Warwicks held up by M.G. and artillery fire and Germans standing on their parapet. These were manned by guns of No 4, No 3 Sections. 3 Lewis gun (of 6) of a piece (?) which although hard fighting the guns of No IV Section did not last 11 minutes as to attempt no advance with the minimum of men impossible, I gave orders that they were to bring the enemy bombers which this section much as possible. On reaching our right I found the Lewis guns had died & old Germans (having 5) them coming over to surrender) working up the ? towards our rear ? indicated by C.S.M. (C.S.M. T. Milne) to ask for reinforcements, thing up the ? our guns. The Lewis guns at Masselot had secured some way that Germans had broken through on the left & two guns pressed there ?? to the right.

WAR DIARY or INTELLIGENCE SUMMARY

Army Form C. 2118.

(Erase heading not required.)

Instructions regarding War Diaries and Intelligence Summaries are contained in F. S. Regs., Part II. and the Staff Manual respectively. Title Pages will be prepared in manuscript.

Place	Date	Hour	Summary of Events and Information	Remarks and references to Appendices
			Started about 9.15 pm when the 2 guns of No 1 section reached our left outlay they line left HILLS "A" Coy 20 meters to able to advance 2 guns of No 2 section to advance him as soon as it reached the enemy trenches until it was the Germans 1st line the guns of No 3 section were however the enemy barrage shed down his an attack was countermanded and 4 Coy which had just left the rally point recalled. Ordered all guns to remain in the front line during the night as counter attack was quite probable. Casualties 5 officers wounded 1 O.R. killed 16 wounded 9 missing. Two of our guns were damaged by shell fire in our own lines. Four guns of No 2 section were left in German trenches but certainly two of them were in a badly damaged condition & quite useless. It was quite impossible to bring the guns back as men were bombed and & hopelessly outnumbered & only 2 managed to get back unwounded.	18 M.G.Coy

Army Form C. 2118.

WAR DIARY
or
INTELLIGENCE SUMMARY
(Erase heading not required.)

Instructions regarding War Diaries and Intelligence Summaries are contained in F.S. Regs., Part II. and the Staff Manual respectively. Title Pages will be prepared in manuscript.

18th MGC Coy

Place	Date	Hour	Summary of Events and Information	Remarks and references to Appendices
21·7·16 LE DRUMEZ	→	9:0 am	Ordered to withdraw all guns except guns of No 1 Section (Chapter) suffered no casualties	h.D
			2 left in road line, 1 in E.R.A House & 1 at MASSELOT HOUSE	
	22·7·16	→	All quiet during day	h.D
LE DRUMEZ	23·7·16		A general M.G. conference afterwards followed by aerial tripod drill was held referred given by Section Officer	h.D
do	24·7·16	2:30 pm	Company moved to GAS ALARM POST on LA BASSÉE Road into rest billets	h.D
			Inspection of 2½ Sections and transport by Divisional General transport complimented on smart turnout	
		3:0 pm	1½ Sections arrive from trenches after relief by 163 M.G. Coy.	
do	25·7·16		Company training	h.D
do	26·7·16		do.	h.D
do	27·7·16		do	h.D
do	28		do	h.D
do	29		do	h.D
do	30		Bath Horse show. Coy secured 2·1sts & 2·2nds.	h.D
do	31		Company training	h.D

W Boynton Capt
O.C. 143 M.G. Coy.

Vol 3

WAR DIARY

of

182nd MACHINE GUN COMPANY

August, 1916.

CONFIDENTIAL

Army Form C. 2118.

WAR DIARY
or
INTELLIGENCE SUMMARY
(*Erase heading not required.*)

192 M.G. Coy

Place	Date	Hour	Summary of Events and Information	Remarks and references to Appendices
LE DRUMEZ (M.3.c.3.2.)	1-8-16	2.30pm 6.0 pm	Orders to take over positions in line held by No 184 M.G. Coy. Headquarters established at Farm M.3.c.3.2. Relief completed. 9 Guns in line. In front line { Anojto No - 11, 15, 22, 21 } In reserve + Keeps { WINCHESTER POST. CINEMA HOUSE. MOATED GRANGE. (2 guns) SIGN POST LANE. } Remaining 7 guns in Bde Reserve at LE DRUMEZ. The gun teams carry on with Company Training (Advanced drill, T.A etc).	h.D
do	2-8-16	6.0 AM	Quiet during night. Hun hit by shrapnel. Enemy sent over 12 aerial torpedoes near emplt 22. No casualties. 5500 rounds fired at gaps and enemy back areas.	h.D
do	3-8-16		2850 rounds fired at gaps in wire and at enemy parapet.	h.D

Army Form C. 2118.

WAR DIARY
or
INTELLIGENCE SUMMARY

(Erase heading not required.)

Instructions regarding War Diaries and Intelligence Summaries are contained in F.S. Regs., Part II. and the Staff Manual respectively. Title Pages will be prepared in manuscript.

182 M.G. Coy.

Place	Date	Hour	Summary of Events and Information	Remarks and references to Appendices
LE DRUMEZ	3.8.16	9.0 p.m. 4 & intervals	3000 rounds at communication trench & trolley lines N25 c.6.6 — N25 c.6.2.	nil.
do	4.8.16	5.0 p.m.	Germans listening post dispersed and three snipers silenced. MOATED G RANGE shelled by A.2, about 24 shells fell doing no damage. 3000 rounds fired at M36 c.0.7 to N31 a.0.3 indirect. 3250 " fired at gaps & enemy parapet during night.	nil
do	5.8.16		Nothing to report during day.	
		10.0 p.m.	7750 rounds fired at N31/19.½ from fired M23 d 17½. (indirect) M24 d 8½ from M35 A.9.2. enemy parapet (indirect) gaps and enemy parapet.	nil
		1150		
		4750		
do	6.8.16	5,600	fired at enemy parapet & gaps in wire at intervals during night.	nil
		3,000	fired indirect from M23 d 17½ at following points:—	
			Railway N25 c.0.6 to N31 a.0 9.7½ crossroads N31 a./2.3. BAS POMMEREAU BOIS du BIEZ	With "Clarke + Jarvis" mounting
do	7.9.16		No 4. Section relieved No 1. Section. Relief complete 4.0 p.m. 2500 rounds fired at M30.c.4/13b.a. from M34a 3/4 8/4 indirect at enemy front parapet lines	nil
		2500	enemy communication trenches	

Army Form C. 2118.

WAR DIARY
or
INTELLIGENCE SUMMARY
(Erase heading not required.)

Instructions regarding War Diaries and Intelligence Summaries are contained in F.S. Regs., Part II. and the Staff Manual respectively. Title Pages will be prepared in manuscript.

Place: 132 M.G. Coy

Date	Hour	Summary of Events and Information	Remarks and references to Appendices
7.8.16 (cont'd)		450 rounds fired at enemy front support lines M30b & M24d (indirect)	hd
		4100 enemy's wire and bivouacs	
8.8.16	3.30am	Enemy exploded a very large mine at M30 c.11.4. Gun emplacements No 23 & 22 were blown up in the explosion and the team at No 22 consisting of 1 Sergt & 5 men wiped out. Enemy bombers after the explosion were dispersed by Lewis guns. During the night guns were brought up on either side to cover the crater but there was no attack, the night being very quiet.	hd
		300 rounds fired at enemy parapet & gaps.	
9.8.16		2250 rounds fired at parapet & gaps	hd
10.8.16		4050 do.	hd
11.8.16		2250 do.	hd
12.8.16		3750 do.	
		750 at enemy front line M36.c. and road junction M30d 8/2 7 } Indirect	
		1000 at enemy front line between M30 B 2 8½ and N 19 C 2½ 8½/2 }	
13.8.16		4600 at enemy parapet and gaps	
		2000 at M30 d 6/17 and road from N31 a 9/2 8½ to N31 b 7 1½ } Indirect	hd
		1750 at enemy front support line M24d N19.C.	

Army Form C. 2118.

WAR DIARY
or
INTELLIGENCE SUMMARY
(Erase heading not required.)

Instructions regarding War Diaries and Intelligence Summaries are contained in F.S. Regs., Part II. and the Staff Manual respectively. Title Pages will be prepared in manuscript.

182 M.G. Coy

Place	Date	Hour	Summary of Events and Information	Remarks and references to Appendices
LE DRUMEZ	14.8.16		4000 rounds at enemy parapet and gaps	n.D.
	15-8-16		4550 do	n.D.
			Gun at M34B½.0. fired 1500 indirect at enemy outpost line M30.A.	
			Gun at M23d 17½ fired 1750 indirect at RUE D'ENFER, O.P at N19c.5.0 and from M31d.97. to N25 c. 6.1/4	n.D.
			Quiet during day	n.D.
		6.0pm	Combined artillery and trench mortar bombardment to which enemy replied.	
		6.30		
	16.8.16	6.30pm	Enemy mortars and artillery around NEUVE CHAPELLE very active	
		7.0pm	8250 rounds fired at enemy parapet and gaps in wire.	
			1500 fired indirect at trolley lines S.6.a.29. to S.6.a.5 3/4. } fired at intervals from 10.0 pm to 3.30 am	n.D.
			1000 from S.6.A.45 to S.6.D.5.9½.	
			1000 S.6 D.5.9½ to S.12 A.5.0.	
			and S.6.A.5.3 to S.6.D.5.8.	
	17.8.16		4100 rounds fired at enemy parapet and gaps in wire	
	18.8.16		8550 do	
			2000 indirect at RUE D'ENFER, Mdn PIETRE, M30d 7½ 8 harrowing road to N25 c.6.1.	n.D.

Army Form C. 2118.

WAR DIARY
or
INTELLIGENCE SUMMARY

(Erase heading not required.)

182nd M.G. Coy.

Place	Date	Hour	Summary of Events and Information	Remarks and references to Appendices
LE DRUMEZ	19.8.16		Quiet during day	
		10.30/pm to 10.50	6 guns fired indirect on to German line, front and support. M30b, M24D, N19c and smoke was discharged from our front to cover a raid by 184th Brigade on point N.9 WICK SALIENT. Artillery shelled German line at the same time. Enemy shelled our front line lightly with Shrapnel.	nil
			4000 rounds fired at gaps and enemy parapet.	
	20.8.16	10.0/pm to 1.0 am	6 guns fired indirect on Bois du BIEZ in conjunction with 183 M.G. Coy who had 6 guns firing also. Artillery and M.T.M searched enemy lines in front of Bois. Enemy M.G bullets passed overhead near our guns at M34 b 1.3.0 but were probably meant from the front line. 9000 rounds fired indirect.	nil
	21.8.16		3250 rounds fired at gaps in wire and enemy parapet. 250 fired indirect at M30 A 6.2	nil
	22.8.16		Section officer reports considerable sniping near No.10. Emplacement, sniper not located.	nil
			4600 rounds fired at gaps in wire and parapet. 1000 fired indirect along RUE d'ENFER TRENCHES SEARCHED. 500 fired in long bursts at group of houses N2b c 38. 1000 fired at junction of roads stanzlines M30 D.97	

2449. Wt. W14957/M90 750,000 1/16 J.B.C. & A. Forms/C.2118/12.

Army Form C. 2118.

WAR DIARY
or
INTELLIGENCE SUMMARY

(Erase heading not required.)

182nd M.G. COY.

Place	Date	Hour	Summary of Events and Information	Remarks and references to Appendices
LE DRUMEZ	23.8.16		5500 fired at enemy bivouac and wire & working party was dispersed at M.30 A 5.4 over. About 3 pm enemy fuel dumps into MOATED GRANGE, only three were hit and they did no damage. During the day, at intervals - 2000 rounds were fired from M34 b 20 at enemy line between BIRDCAGE and TRIVELET. There was some artillery activity during the night, probably consequent on our M.T.M. bombardment.	M.D.
	24.8.16		Quiet during day. To cover the raid by a company of the 8th WARWICKS on German line M36 c 3.8 to M35 a 9.2 five of our guns barraged enemy communication trench M36 Central & N.E. corner of BOIS du BIEZ in conjunction with artillery & Stokes guns. 4400 rounds fired indirect from M34 b ½.0, M27 b 9.2¾ and M28 d ½.8 ½. So far as our M.Gs were concerned there was no enemy retaliation, though many M.G. bullets passed over guns at M28 d 7.8 ½ - probably ours fired at our front line. After raid enemy's M.Gs were very active. Enemy did slight damage to an open emplacement when called upon by his own infantry for support. 3400 rounds were fired at safe in wire and at enemy parapet.	M.D.

Army Form C. 2118.

WAR DIARY
or
INTELLIGENCE SUMMARY

(Erase heading not required.)

Instructions regarding War Diaries and Intelligence Summaries are contained in F. S. Regs., Part II. and the Staff Manual respectively. Title Pages will be prepared in manuscript.

Place	Date	Hour	Summary of Events and Information	Remarks and references to Appendices
LEDREUMEZ	25.8.16		182nd M.G. Coy. 3500 rounds fired at gaps in enemy wire and parapet.	
do	26.8.16		Relieved by No 183 M.G. Coy (Capt WALKER) Relief complete 7.0 pm. Company proceeded to rest billets at LESTREM R.2.C.9.8. Transport lines R.2.D.8.8.	N.D
	27.8.16		⎫	
	28.8.16		⎬ Company training. Range being constructed. Rain	N.D
	29.8.16		⎭	
	30.8.16			
	31.8.16			

M Douglas Capt.
O.C. 182nd M.G. Coy.

Confidential.

Vol 4

War Diary
of
182nd Machine Gun Coy.

From 1.9.16. to 20.9.16.

(Volume 5)

Army Form C. 2118.

WAR DIARY
or
INTELLIGENCE SUMMARY
(Erase heading not required.)

Instructions regarding War Diaries and Intelligence Summaries are contained in F. S. Regs., Part II. and the Staff Manual respectively. Title Pages will be prepared in manuscript.

182nd M.G. Coy.

Place	Date	Hour	Summary of Events and Information	Remarks and references to Appendices
LESTREM	1/9/16		Company training.	n.D
do	2/9/16		do	n.D
LAVENTIE	3/9/16	8.30am	Company started to relieve No 184 M.G Coy in the FAUQUISSART Sector.	
		12:30	Relief complete. Guns at following points :— 4 in front line 1 MASSELOT HOUSE 1 C.R.A. HOUSE 1 JOCKS LODGE 1 FAUQUISSART POST. 1 FLANK POST. 1 COPSE. 6 guns in RESERVE at LAVENTIE.	n.D
			2750 rounds fired at gaps in wire and enemy parapet.	n.D
do	4.9.16		5500 fired (1500 indirect) at enemy wire. Fire held up during afternoon & night owing to patrols being out. Some sniping reported near FAUQUISSART Post — probably bullets intended for front line.	n.D
do	5.9.16		4250 rounds fired direct at enemy parapet and gaps. 1500 enfilading his wire and parapet (fired indirect). FAUQUISSART POST shelled on night of 4/5th but emplacement was not damaged.	n.D

WAR DIARY
or
INTELLIGENCE SUMMARY
(Erase heading not required.)

Army Form C. 2118.

182nd M.G. Coy.

Place	Date	Hour	Summary of Events and Information	Remarks and references to Appendices
LAVENTIE	6.9.16		5500 rounds fired at enemy wire and parapet.	h.D.
			1250 rounds fired in cooperation with M.T.M.'s between N.8.D.2½.1½ and N.8.D.2½.2.0 (inclusive)	
		1300	at SUGAR LOAF and enfilading German line EASTWARDS between	
		5/pm and 10/pm.		
			FLANK POST shelled with 4.2 during day	
			FAUQUISSART POST again shelled.	
do	7.9.16		Firing held up part of night owing to 3 raids on brigade front	
			3750 rounds fired at parapet and wire. During day bursts were fired over parapet with hyposcope along enemy parapet to hook (?) snipers etc. Good observation was obtained by men in the flanks with periscopes. The firing drew no retaliation	h.D.
			Indirect fire was brought on enemy front support lines during the day from the SUGAR LOAF eastwards; bursts of 50 rounds were fired at frequent intervals.	
			2000 rounds fired	
do	8.9.16		4600 rounds fired at wire and parapet.	
			750 indirect at N.9.c.1¼.1½ — N.9.c.6.1 } In conjunction with 15th Australian Bde	h.D.
			750 do at N.15.a.1½.9½ — N.15.a.6.8¼ }	
			2500 do at RUE d'ENTER in conjunction with 183rd Infy Bde	
			The concrete (?) of one of our emplacements was found on examination in No-Man's-Land to be cracked and was covered with earth.	

Army Form C. 2118.

WAR DIARY
or
INTELLIGENCE SUMMARY
(Erase heading not required.)

182nd M.G. Coy.

Place	Date	Hour	Summary of Events and Information	Remarks and references to Appendices
LAVENTIE	9.9.16		5100 rounds fired direct — at wire and parapet. An especially fast wire was used and good observation obtained. 1500 rounds fired indirect at N14 D½ 2.2 by day and night. 1500 — at N8 d 2 1½ to N9 c 9.1. An infantry raid was assisted during the night by keeping fire on an enemy sap.	nil
do	10.9.16		3500 rounds fired direct. 1500 indirect Eastwards from SUGARLOAF. Enemy blew in the top of PICANTIN AVENUE with H.T.M. doing no damage otherwise. An enemy working party was discovered about N 8 c. 5. 3, later the horns calling ambulance men were heard and it is presumed that some of the working party were hit. MASSELOT HOUSE was lit up by M.Gs firing indirect — probably searching for Rue MASSELOT enemy	nil
do	11.9.16		5200 rounds fired direct at wire and parapet. An enemy working party was dispersed at 11.0pm at N13d 2.5. 3000 rounds fired indirect at N19c 1.6½. 1100 rounds fired indirect Eastwards from Sugar loaf.	
do	12.9.16		3550 fired direct at parapet and wire. 2500 indirect at SUGARLOAF and eastwards N14 D½.4½ — N20B.1.9. 2000 — at new trench (not shown on map) N14 D½.4½ — N20B 3.4½. 2150 indirect N14 D 1.0 to N20 B 3.4½.	nil

Army Form C. 2118.

WAR DIARY
or
INTELLIGENCE SUMMARY
(Erase heading not required.)

182nd M.G. Coy.

Instructions regarding War Diaries and Intelligence Summaries are contained in F. S. Regs., Part II. and the Staff Manual respectively. Title Pages will be prepared in manuscript.

Place	Date	Hour	Summary of Events and Information	Remarks and references to Appendices
LAVENTIE	12.9.16		The indirect fire employed would seem to be doing harm to the enemy as whenever fire was opened an enemy gun replied searching for ours.	
do	13.9.16		5000 rounds fired at enemy loophole and wire by night (See rounds fired over loophole with Hyposcope during day)	S.D.
			1500 indirect at SUGAR LOAF and Eastwards enfilading German front & Supports	
			2250 indirect fired at trenches during night N14 C 2.4½ — N20 A 9½.7½	
			An enemy working party was fired on at N14 a 7.3½	
			Two enemy machine guns are reputed to be ranging by firing single shots	
			3750 rounds fired at gaps and parapet.	
do	14.9.16		3000 fired indirect from N19 C 3.2 to N25 B.b.o. by night	
			2750 fired indirect from N8 D 4½.1½ to N9 c 9.1 by day	
			2500 fired indirect from N20 B 3½.½ to N21 C ½.2½ by night	hed
			high reported very good. MASSELOT STREET shelled a little during day.	
do	15.9.16		5000 fired direct at wire + gaps	
			2500 fired indirect at new trench (not on map) crossing RUE DELEVAL about N20 b.1½.9 by night traversing + searching	
			3000 fired indirect Eastwards of SUGAR LOAF	

WAR DIARY
or
INTELLIGENCE SUMMARY
(Erase heading not required.)

Army Form C. 2118.

Instructions regarding War Diaries and Intelligence Summaries are contained in F.S. Regs., Part II. and the Staff Manual respectively. Title Pages will be prepared in manuscript.

82nd M.G. Coy.

Place	Date	Hour	Summary of Events and Information	Remarks and references to Appendices
LAVENTIE	15.9.16		A tall tree at COPSE POST (N.7.c.2½.7) which is fitted with ladder and cradle has been employed as an O.P. A telephone is fixed from the cradle to the gun (near the post of the tree) and an observer has been hoisted with a libo rope. He has been unable to obtain observation of our fire and has — during the last week — seen nothing on to which he could advantageously direct a M.G. Today 2 shots were fired at officers observing from this tree and it has probably been "spotted" by the Germans. If must be visible from the German Support line with glasses.	n.O.
do	16.9.16		5750 rounds fired direct at enemy parapet and wire. Several belts were discharged at suspected snipers posts with Hyscope during the day showing an occasional shot from sniper. 1250 rounds fired indirect at N13d 2¼.4 to N13d 9.6) in conjunction with M.T.M's and 1000 rounds fired indirect at N13d 2—½ to N13d 2¼.2) 6" hows. 3000 rounds fired indirect eastwards from SUGAR BAT. Night quiet and nothing to report during day. A "listen how" baulked from 12.0 noon to 12.30 pm with M.T.M's, 6" hows & M.Gs drew no retaliation from the enemy.	n.D.

2449 Wt. W14957/M90 750,000 1/16 J.B.C. & A. Forms/C.2118/12.

Army Form C. 2118.

WAR DIARY
or
INTELLIGENCE SUMMARY
(Erase heading not required.)

Instructions regarding War Diaries and Intelligence Summaries are contained in F. S. Regs., Part II. and the Staff Manual respectively. Title Pages will be prepared in manuscript.

Place	Date	Hour	Summary of Events and Information	Remarks and references to Appendices
LAVENTIE	17.9.16		182nd M.G. Coy.	
			5250 rounds fired direct at enemy parapet and wire. During day trench mirror fixed over parapet at Snipers loophole, periscopes etc.	n.d.
			1000 indirect at N13d 2.4 to N13d.0.3	
			1000 indirect at N13d 2-½ to N13d 4¾-2. } In conjunction with T.M.'s	
			1000 indirect at N13d 3½.4 to N13d 9.5	
			Enemy sent over a few Aerial torpedoes on the left doing no damage	
	18.9.16		4800 rounds fired direct at enemy parapet & wire.	n.d.
			500 indirect at N13c.8.0 to N13D.c.3.	
			3000 indirect at N19c.5.0 to N25B 6½.0	
			500 indirect at N19A.0.6¾ to N19.c. 0.6½	
			1000 indirect at N13d 6½ traversing to N14.c 2½.7.	
			Night reported quiet	
	19.9.16		6020 rounds fired at enemy parapet & wire.	n.d.
			1250 fired indirect at N13d 1½.2 to N13 d 3½.3½. In conjunction with T.M.s	
			1800 fired indirect at Kens trench N14 Bq 2½. to N14 B 8½.7½ and traversing	
			1250 fired indirect at N14 c½.3½.	
			Enemy M.G.s started firing indirect about MASSELDT HOUSE, and M.G.'s generally very active during early morning	

Army Form C. 2118.

WAR DIARY
or
INTELLIGENCE SUMMARY
(Erase heading not required.)

192nd M.G. Coy.

Place	Date	Hour	Summary of Events and Information	Remarks and references to Appendices
LAVENTIE	20.9.16		5000 rounds fired direct at wire and parapet. Several bursts were fired with Hyposcopes during the day.	hw
		2000	indirect from N.9.a.4.10.9.11 on tracks to	
		1500	indirect N.14.D.8½.5½ to N.21.A.6.6.	
		2250	indirect N.19.A.4.3 to N.19.B.4.0. In conjunction with M.T.M's on Wick Salient	
			Enemy reply to our T.M. bombardment consisted of about 15 Shrapnel near FAUQUISSART POST.	
			Day and night quiet. Enemy seems to take our T.M. bombardments very quietly and his retaliation is neither as great nor as effective and was	
do	21.9.16	6150	rounds fired direct at wire and parapet. A single gun was showing the L.K. of the parapet at N.19.A.31.b were fired on during the day with good results.	hw
		2500	indirect N.20.d.9½.9¼ to N.21.C.4½.3½ by night.	
		3500	indirect N.14.C.74.4.6 common margin tracks hacks known as enemy aeroplane flares are believed to be used by parties working on new front line	

WAR DIARY or INTELLIGENCE SUMMARY

Army Form C. 2118.

Place	Date	Hour	Summary of Events and Information	Remarks and references to Appendices
LAVENTIE	22.9.16		No 182 M.G. Coy.	
			6000 rounds fired direct at gaps and parapet. Several shots fired at enemy haulpt during the day.	
		2300	fired indirect N14.c.1.3 to N14.D.8½.8.	
		1000	fired indirect N20.c.3.5 to along road running S.E. in bursts during night	hrD
			4 Shells dropped near MASSELOT HOUSE during day, probably owing to a working party being seen by enemy. Enemy aeroplanes rather more active than usual; they were run down in the early morning at a very great height and present no target for M.G.s	
do	23.9.16		5,250 rounds fired direct at parapet & loopholes.	
		2000	rounds indirect at Germans line N19.A.7. to about N19.c.0.6½. enfilade. during day & night.	hrD
		500	rounds indirect enfilading German line EAST of SUGAR LOAF	
		3750	rounds indirect at trolley lines running S.E from N14.c.2.4.	
			Enemy sent over Shells near FAUQUISSART POST at 1.15 p.m. in reply to our T.M's. Night and day very quiet.	

Army Form C. 2118.

WAR DIARY
or
INTELLIGENCE SUMMARY
(Erase heading not required.)

Instructions regarding War Diaries and Intelligence Summaries are contained in F.S. Regs., Part II. and the Staff Manual respectively. Title Pages will be prepared in manuscript.

182nd M.G. Coy.

Place	Date	Hour	Summary of Events and Information	Remarks and references to Appendices
LAVENTIE	24.9.16		4250 rounds fired indirect at enemy peaceful service. 2500 fired indirect at new trench crossing RUE DELEVAL during night. 1250 fired indirect at enemy trench front N19A4½.7½ enfilade. During the afternoon several hundred rounds were fired at the new Enemy trench & an attempt to obtain observation made. This was quite unsuccessful. Infantry had patrols out during the greater part of the night, which were very quiet.	nil
LAVENTIE	25.9.16		7000 rounds fired direct at peaceful and wire. 1000 indirect N19c34.1½ testically searching road. 2750 indirect at enemy trenches N19A4½7 and tramlines N19A2½4½. Two working parties were fired on and dispersed but it was too misty to observe whether casualties were caused. Several shells fell in the vicinity of MASSELOT HOUSE doing no damage (77 m.m During morning a figure reported enemy sniper near N19A 3.2. We mounted a gun on the house (with disappearing mounting - Guthrie ([?])) and with our sniper as observer fired 25.8 at the target. Two belts were fired quickly, 400 rounds were a specified "target". The loophole must have been pierced many times.	nil

2449 Wt. W14957/M90 750,000 1/16 J.B.C. & A. Forms/C.2118/12.

Army Form C. 2118.

WAR DIARY
or
INTELLIGENCE SUMMARY
(Erase heading not required.)

182nd M.G. Coy.

Place	Date	Hour	Summary of Events and Information	Remarks and references to Appendices
LAVENTIE.	26/9/16		4750 fired direct at wire and enemy parapet	
			1000 indirect at N20 A 9¼ 7½.	
			Night and day very quiet and uneventful. The Germans does not often even retaliate when we start a bombardment and never indulge in one of himself.	nil
			His M.G's firing indirect on 25% killed a man at COPSE POST but otherwise have been singularly inactive.	
do	27/9/16		6250 rounds fired direct at gaps in enemy parapet	
			2000 indirect fired at road N27 B.5.7.	
			Night very quiet. Enemy either very weak or doing much work behind lines as few Germans are visible.	nil
do	28/9/16		10380 rounds fired at enemy wire and parapet.	
			1000 rounds indirect at N20 A.5.8 tramlines (during night)	
			8000 rounds indirect fired from 9.0 pm to 10 am at roads leading into AUBERS— N26c.6.6½. N26b.6¼.1¼. N27 or 3.4¼ and road running from N26c 8½.3½. to N27a 5½.2.	nil
			This indirect fire was intended to catch hand parties going up to the trenches.	

Army Form C. 2118.

WAR DIARY
or
INTELLIGENCE SUMMARY
(Erase heading not required.)

Instructions regarding War Diaries and Intelligence Summaries are contained in F. S. Regs., Part II. and the Staff Manual respectively. Title Pages will be prepared in manuscript.

Place	Date	Hour	Summary of Events and Information	Remarks and references to Appendices
LAVENTIE	28.9.16		which end at these roads. Our guns opened fire simultaneously and fired a couple of 50 round bursts, the Germans thought an infantry raid was being covered with M.G. fire and retaliated on own wire. No retaliation was caused.	
do	29.9.16		7000 rounds fired at gaps and enemy parapet. 1000 indirect N.9.a.6/L.5 to N.9.c.6/4/2½. After shells fell near C.R.A.'s house in the afternoon light very good.	h.D
do	30.9.16		6500 rounds fired at enemy wire and parapet. 3000 indirect N.9.a.4.6 to N.9.c.4.2.5.2 500 indirect Eastwards from S.M.R. HAT. The enemy artillery was slightly more active but was silenced by our own artillery.	h.D

M Boyles Capt.
O.C. 182nd M.G. Coy

2449 Wt. W14957/M90 750,000 1/16 J.B.C. & A. Forms/C.2118/12.

Army Form C. 2118.

WAR DIARY
or
INTELLIGENCE SUMMARY

(Erase heading not required.)

Instructions regarding War Diaries and Intelligence Summaries are contained in F. S. Regs, Part II. and the Staff Manual respectively. Title Pages will be prepared in manuscript.

183rd M.G. Coy

Place	Date	Hour	Summary of Events and Information	Remarks and references to Appendices
LAVENTIE.	1.10.16		wounded	
			8000 direct at gaps in wire and enemy parapet during night	
		1970	indirect fired N19A.5.7 to N19C.4.5.	
			An infantry raid taking place, we guns in the front line co-operated with the attacking party by firing on the flanks. Raid very successful. 20 enemy killed & prisoner.	hid
			During the afternoon our T.M's drew some light retaliation on RUE TILLELOY, FAUQUISSART and MASSELOT TRENCH.	
do	2.10.16		5000 fired direct at wire & parapet by night.	
		2000	indirect fired N19A.5.7. to N19.c.3.2.	
			During the morning an enemy sniper was located about N13d.11.4's. A gun was mounted with about ½ hour's mounting in YOULTEN HYPOCafe and an observer posted with a No.14. Periscope. 500 rounds were fired at the loophole plate, knocking it back but not piercing it. As the sniper was behind the plate when we opened fire and the sandbags did not appear bulletproof it is possible that he was wounded.	hid

2449 Wt. W14957/M90 750,000 1/16 J.B.C. & A. Forms/C.2118/12.

Army Form C. 2118.

WAR DIARY
or
INTELLIGENCE SUMMARY
(Erase heading not required.)

182nd M.G. Coy

Instructions regarding War Diaries and Intelligence Summaries are contained in F.S. Regs., Part II. and the Staff Manual respectively. Title Pages will be prepared in manuscript.

Place	Date	Hour	Summary of Events and Information	Remarks and references to Appendices
LAVENTIE	3.10.16		4400 rounds fired direct at enemy parapet & wire by night	
			1000 rounds fired at German front line EAST of the SUGAR LOAF by daylight (enfilade)	
			3000 rounds fired indirect by night at tramlines N14.C.1¾.4½ — N20.A.9½.7½	
			3000 rounds fired indirect by night at tramlines along RUE d'ENFER N19.C.½.3¾ — N25.B.B.O.	Nil
			3000 rounds fired indirect by day along German line (enfiladed) N19.A.4.5 — M19.C.3.3	
			During the afternoon twenty artillery shells fell on the right hand of WINCHESTER TRENCH. 75% were unfired	
	4.10.16		Day & night otherwise very quiet	
			5500 rounds fired direct at enemy wire and parapet during night	
			2750 indirect fired EAST of SUGAR LOAF	
			2000 indirect N19.A.5½.7¾ — N19.A.4½.3¾	
			2500 indirect N.14.C.7.4 — head of new German communication trench	Nil
			Night and day very quiet and nothing unusual to report	

Army Form C. 2118.

WAR DIARY
or
INTELLIGENCE SUMMARY

(Erase heading not required.)

Instructions regarding War Diaries and Intelligence Summaries are contained in F. S. Regs., Part II. and the Staff Manual respectively. Title Pages will be prepared in manuscript.

182nd M.G. Coy

Place	Date	Hour	Summary of Events and Information	Remarks and references to Appendices
LAVENTIE	5/10/16		5250 rounds fired direct at enemy wire and parapet.	
			3250 indirect fired from COPSE & filalading enemy road & support line EAST of SUGAR LOAF by day & night.	
			3000 indirect enfilading German line M19A 5¼, 7¼ — M19.C.2½.3¾.day & night	h.W
			5000 indirect fired from 7.30 pm to 12.30 am at roads leading into AUBERS	
			Enemy put about 15 77 mm shells into M24.6 doing no damage. These evidently came from an enfilade battery	
			day & night very quiet.	
			Germans seem to be doing a good deal of work behind their front line which appears very much knocked about. Several trains were observed in AUBERS which to naked eye curiously seem stalling about as though they know we they could not be observed.	
do	6/10/16		5850 rounds fired direct at wire and parapet	
			3000 indirect N19a 5¼ 7¾ — N19.C.2½.3.5¾ by day & night	
			3250 indirect EASTWARDS from SUGAR LOAF (altitude)	h.W
			Enemy artillery slightly more active but no return of damage done. Enemy working party observed about M19A 8.5 at back one man was lit through when not known	

Army Form C. 2118.

WAR DIARY
or
INTELLIGENCE SUMMARY
(Erase heading not required.)

192nd M.G. Coy.

Place	Date	Hour	Summary of Events and Information	Remarks and references to Appendices
LAVENTIE	7.9.16		5100 rounds fired direct at gaps and enemy parapet 2500 indirect N20 A 97 } 250 " N19D24.34 – N19D8½0 } To support an infantry raid 2500 " N25n.7.7½ Fire was splendid in support of the raid and no response to the artillery fire and was continued until the conclusion of the raid. The raid was successful in gaining identifications. Enemy artillery and Minenwerfe fairly active.	M.O.
	8.9.16		4250 Rounds fired direct at enemy parapet and gaps in wire. 1000 rounds were fired over the parapet with a M/V of 1450f at 1260 muzzle at a German another post. The top field was hundred in and the sand bags round it were cut to bits. The guns were mounted in the parapet. Day & night very quiet and nothing to report.	M.O.

Army Form C. 2118.

WAR DIARY
or
INTELLIGENCE SUMMARY
(Erase heading not required.)

192nd M.G. Coy.

Place	Date	Hour	Summary of Events and Information	Remarks and references to Appendices
LAVENTIE	9.10.16		6000 rounds fired direct at gaps and enemy trenches during night.	
			1500 indirect by day+night enfilading German line EAST of SUGAR LOAF.	
			2000 indirect at N20B.2½.3¾ v N21A.6½.5½.	
			1000 indirect N14b.5½.1. - N15A.2.6.	
			2000 indirect N19.C.4.1. along Rue d' ENFER.	
			Enemy artillery more active than it has recently been. Nothing further to report.	
	10.10.16		5000 rounds fired direct at enemy wire & trenches.	
			1500 indirect fired by Day EAST OF SUGAR LOAF.	
			Day quieter than usual.	
	11.10.16		5100 rounds fired direct at enemy wire & trenches.	
			1500 indirect enfilading GERMAN line EAST OF SUGAR LOAF.	
			1500 indirect N14b.1½.	
			Emplacement at N14G.2.3½ was flown in by light T.M.	
			Enemy artillery +T.M.S more active especially near RED LAMP.	

Army Form C. 2118.

WAR DIARY
or
INTELLIGENCE SUMMARY
(Erase heading not required.)

182nd M.G Coy

Place	Date	Hour	Summary of Events and Information	Remarks and references to Appendices
LAVENTIE	12.10.16		5000 rounds fired direct at enemy wire and enemy parapet. 1750 indirect at German line EAST of SUGAR LOAF 2000 indirect at new trench (where damaged by H.S.Mor) about N20.B.4.4. by night 3000 indirect at enemy communication trench M19.D.2/4.5/2 – M19.D.3/4.0 Enemy artillery active round S.ELGIN & ERITH TRENCHES Nothing of interest to report	nil
do	13.10.16		5500 rounds fired direct at enemy wire & parapet. 1500 fired indirect at enemy hd EAST of SUGAR LOAF Morning quiet. Afternoon enemy in reply to M.T.M's shelled our line rather heavily	nil
do	14.10.16		5450 rounds fired direct at gaps in wire & enemy parapet. 2000 indirect N15 A 8/4.6. — N15.a.9.6 with an occasional tap on to the road. 3000 indirect N25.B.5.5 1500 indirect EAST of SUGAR LOAF. 3000 indirect at trenches & light railway around N14.c.1/2.5/2. Our coy at N14a 2/4.3 has been subjected to rather a lot of light T.M. fire	nil

Army Form C. 2118.

WAR DIARY
or
INTELLIGENCE SUMMARY
(Erase heading not required.)

Instructions regarding War Diaries and Intelligence Summaries are contained in F. S. Regs., Part II. and the Staff Manual respectively. Title Pages will be prepared in manuscript.

182nd M.G. Coy.

Place	Date	Hour	Summary of Events and Information	Remarks and references to Appendices
LAVENTIE	15/10/16		5000 rounds fired direct at gaps in wire & enemy parapet.	nil.
			2000 indirect N15a.8/4.6 — N15a.9.6.	
			2000 indirect N14.C.½.2/2.	
			1000 indirect N35.B.5.5.	
			2000 indirect N8d 3/2.2 — N9.c.o 5/4.	
			Day & night very quiet. nothing to report.	
do	16/10/16		5250 rounds fired direct at gaps in wire & enemy parapet	nil
			1500 indirect N8D 3/½ 2 — N9.C.O 5/4.	
			2000 indirect N14.C. ½.2/2	
			6 enemy aeroplanes rather active; 5 crossing the lights of the Bde front.	
do	17/10/16		4500 rounds fired direct at enemy parapet & gaps in wire.	nil
			2000 indirect at N14.C. ½ — 2/2	
			1500 indirect at SUGAR LOAF and EASTWARDS.	
			12,000 indirect at roads leading into & out of AUBERS, fired from guns mounted immediately behind the parapet in the front line.	

WAR DIARY or INTELLIGENCE SUMMARY

Army Form C. 2118.

183rd M.G. Coy.

Place	Date	Hour	Summary of Events and Information	Remarks and references to Appendices
LAVENTIE	18.10.16		5500 rounds fired direct at enemy parapet. Enemy shelled Rue Tilleloy in reply to our M.T.M's. Enemy M.G's active during night.	nil
do	19.10.16		6250 rounds fired direct at enemy parapet. 3000 rounds fired indirect N26.6.5/3.5/4. Night reported exceptionally quiet.	nil
do	20.10.16		6000 rounds fired direct at gaps in enemy wire & parapet. A.A. Beating Officer on our left reported that a ground M.G. hit a Hun Patrol as one of his own patrols heard shrieks & groans. Several "duds" fell near to the hedge. Enemy aeroplanes very active but flying at a great height.	nil
do	21.10.16		3500 rounds fired direct at enemy wire & parapet. 1000 indirect fired N25.14.5.9 / N25.B.3.2. 2500 indirect fired N30.B.4.0. — N30 D.9.4. Enemy M.G very active covering our parapet. Very quiet, nothing of importance noted on the listening apparatus. Glycerine mist on listening apparatus gets furry.	nil

Army Form C. 2118.

WAR DIARY
or
INTELLIGENCE SUMMARY
(Erase heading not required.)

182nd M.G. Coy

Place	Date	Hour	Summary of Events and Information	Remarks and references to Appendices
LAVENTIE	22.10.16		5250 rounds fired direct at enemy wire from a.k.k.	nil
			1500 indirect N26 A 2.7¾ — N26 A 4.5 ¾	
			nothing to report. Day + night quiet.	
LAVENTIE	23.10.16		4500 rounds fired direct at enemy wire from a.k.k.	nil
			Very quiet uneventful.	
do	24.10.16		4500 rounds fired direct at gaps in wire enemy parapet	
			500 rounds fired indirect N13 D 8¾.5 — N14 C 1.5 ¾/4	
			750 rounds fired indirect N 19 A 3.3½ — N19 A 3.0. In conjunction with a dummy raid	
			5 minutes rapid fire was used from each gun at the enemy front line on either side of point of entry; this was intended to call the	nil
			enemy living his parapet.	
			Day quiet uneventful.	

Army Form C. 2118.

WAR DIARY
or
INTELLIGENCE SUMMARY
(Erase heading not required.)

Instructions regarding War Diaries and Intelligence Summaries are contained in F. S. Regs., Part II. and the Staff Manual respectively. Title Pages will be prepared in manuscript.

182nd M.G. Coy.

Place	Date	Hour	Summary of Events and Information	Remarks and references to Appendices
LAVENTIE	25.10.16		3750 rounds fired direct at enemy wire & henefel. Day & night quiet.	nil.
do	26.10.16		5000 rounds fired direct at enemy wire & henefel. 3000 rounds fired indirect along RUE d'ENFER. 3000 rounds fired indirect down BERTHA TRENCH and railway running alongside. Day & night quiet.	nil.
do	27.10.16		3300 rounds fired direct at enemy henefel trow. Very heavy rain during day. Enemy must have expected relief as he was more active than usual. Quiet during night. 10 guns of 168 M.G. Coy went into front line & guns but did not take over line from us.	nil.
do	28.10.16		Company relieved by 168 M.G. Coy. Relief completed - no incident - by 12 noon made for H.Q. on right. Enemy showed great activity and undoubtedly got word of the relief. Company moved into billets at ESTAIRES	nil.

2449 Wt. W14957/M90 750,000 1/16 J.B.C. & A. Forms/C.2118/12.

Army Form C. 2118.

WAR DIARY
or
INTELLIGENCE SUMMARY
(Erase heading not required.)

182nd M.G. Coy.

Place	Date	Hour	Summary of Events and Information	Remarks and references to Appendices
ESTAIRES	29/10/16		Company moved from ESTAIRES to MERVILLE.	nil
MERVILLE	30/10/16		Company training.	nil
MERVILLE	31/10/16		do	nil
			do	nil

M Brylino Capt.
O.C. 182 M.G. Coy

Vol 6

Confidential

War Diary
of
182nd Machine Gun Company

From Nov. 1st 1916 to Nov. 30th 1916

Army Form C. 2118.

WAR DIARY
or
INTELLIGENCE SUMMARY

(Erase heading not required.)

Instructions regarding War Diaries and Intelligence Summaries are contained in F. S. Regs., Part II. and the Staff Manual respectively. Title Pages will be prepared in manuscript.

182nd M.G. Coy.

Place	Date	Hour	Summary of Events and Information	Remarks and references to Appendices
MERVILLE	1.11.16		Company training	h.D
MERVILLE	2.11.16		marched to GONNEHEM	h.D
GONNEHEM	3.11.16		marched to Auchel (AUCHEL)	h.D
AUCHEL	4.11.16		marched to OSTREVILLE	h.D
OSTREVILLE	5.11.16		marched to CANNETTEMONT	h.D
CANNETTEMONT	6.11.16		marched to BEAUVOIR	h.D
BEAUVOIR	7.11.16		Company training	h.D
do	8.11.16		do	h.D
do	9.11.16		do	h.D
do	10.11.16		do	h.D
do	11.11.16		do	h.D
do	12.11.16		do	h.D
do	13.11.16		do	h.D
do	14.11.16		do	h.D
do	15.11.16		marched to BERNEVIL	h.D
BERNEVIL	16.11.16		marched to BERTEAUCOURT	h.D
BERTEAUCOURT	17.11.16		marched to RUBEMPRE	h.D

Army Form C. 2118.

WAR DIARY
or
INTELLIGENCE SUMMARY

(Erase heading not required.)

Instructions regarding War Diaries and Intelligence Summaries are contained in F. S. Regs., Part II. and the Staff Manual respectively. Title Pages will be prepared in manuscript.

182nd M.G. Coy.

Place	Date	Hour	Summary of Events and Information	Remarks and references to Appendices
RUBEMPRE	18-11-16		Marched to WARLOY.	A.D.
WARLOY	19-11-16		Rested at WARLOY.	A.D.
WARLOY	20-11-16		- do -	A.D.
WARLOY	21-11-16		Marched to ALBERT.	A.D.
ALBERT	22-11-16		Marched to SENLIS	A.D.
SENLIS	23-11-16		Company training	A.D.
do	24-11-16		- do -	A.D.
do	25-11-16		- do -	A.D.
do	26-11-16		- do -	A.D.
do	27-11-16		Marched to HEDAUVILLE	A.D.
HEDAUVILLE	28-11-16		Company training	A.D.
	29-11-16		- do -	A.D.
	30-11-16		- do -	A.D.

J.J. Goble K.
F. O.G. Cor
O.C. 182 M.G. Cor

Vol 7

CONFIDENTIAL

No. 182 MACHINE GUN COMPANY.
-o-o-o-o-o-o-o-

W A R   D I A R Y

DECEMBER 1ST 1916 to DECEMBER 31ST 1916.

(VOLUME 7)

Army Form C. 2118.

WAR DIARY
or
INTELLIGENCE SUMMARY

(Erase heading not required.)

Instructions regarding War Diaries and Intelligence Summaries are contained in F. S. Regs., Part II. and the Staff Manual respectively. Title Pages will be prepared in manuscript.

Place	Date	Hour	Summary of Events and Information	Remarks and references to Appendices
HEDAUVILLE	1.12.16		Company training	
do	2.12.16		do	
MARTINSART	3.12.16		BdC moved up to support. Company training	
do	4.12.16		Company training	
do	5.12.16		do	
do	6.12.16		do	
do	7.12.16		do	
do	8.12.16		do	
do	9.12.16		do	
do	10.1.16		Bombing moved up into trenches 153rd M.G. Coy. bey Hq at MOUQUET FARM. 18 guns in the line but none in front of REGINA TRENCH.	

General (Approximately) following positions:–
R20.d.99. R22.c.1.9. R22.b.65. R23.0.hu R22.b.8½.9½
R21.a.2.0. R22.c.2.7. R23.b.5.8. R23.a.1.J R22.b.8½.9½
R21.d.3.6. R25.b.58. R23.b.4.2.
R21.d.9.0. R22.a.9.8½ R23.b.4.2.

Guns have all dugout dugouts (in three cases dugouts but no dugout) Infects mounted by day & night with sentry. Guns kept in dugout heavily sunny from being on the forward slope & a heavy is in view of the enemy.

Relief complete by 9 p.m.

Army Form C. 2118.

WAR DIARY
or
INTELLIGENCE SUMMARY
(Erase heading not required.)

182nd M.G. Coy

Place	Date	Hour	Summary of Events and Information	Remarks and references to Appendices
MOUQUET FARM.	11.12.16		Intermittent shelling during day. No dugouts are all old German dugouts any movement from them attracts shell fire. Be first about 3000 yards.	h.D.
do	12.12.16		Usual shelling. Indirect fire from two guns into GRANDCOURT and approaches to MIRAUMONT at night.	h.D.
do	13.12.16		Usual artillery activity.	h.D.
do	14.12.16		do. Indirect fire on BULLESCOURT FARM.	h.D.
do	15.12.16		do. Salvage work done, each man carrying to dgts bringing in some article of equipment with him. Germans in line occupied will improving dugouts, emplacements & hanging dead.	h.D.
do	16.12.16		Artillery fairly active. Indirect fire on roads & tracks leading into MIRAUMONT.	h.D.
do	17.12.16		Usual shelling. Enemy seems to be sending over a shrapnel & H.E. shell together, the H.E. shell bursting about 100 yards in rear of shrapnel. Shells used almost exclusively 5.9" & 4.2"	h.D.
do	18.12.16		Artillery fire normal. Indirect fire on GRANDCOURT & MIRAUMONT.	h.D.

WAR DIARY
or
INTELLIGENCE SUMMARY

(Erase heading not required.)

Army Form C. 2118.

162nd M.G. Coy

Place	Date	Hour	Summary of Events and Information	Remarks and references to Appendices
MOUQUET FARM	19/12/16		German M.G. salved from dugout in STUMP ROAD about R21.A.7.2.½.	h.D
do	20/11/16		No 4 gun M.G.C. No. 10 gun. No. 10 gun in excellent order & evidently not been used. Shelling around.	h.D
			Company relieved by 184 M.G.C. Relief began 3.30 p.m. and reported finished by 8.0 p.m. On casualty — the first of the tour — occurred during the relief. Company moved into huts N19.C.	h.D
MARTINSART	21/12/16		Cleaning kits.	—
do	22/12/16		Marched into huts at HEDAUVILLE.	h.D
HEDAUVILLE	23/12/16		Cleaning & fitting harness.	h.D
do	24/12/16		All guns thoroughly tested on range.	h.D
do	25/12/16		Christmas day.	h.D
do	26/12/16		Company training.	h.D
do	27/12/16		do	h.D
do	28/12/16		do	h.D
do	29/12/16		do	h.D

Army Form C. 2118.

WAR DIARY
or
INTELLIGENCE SUMMARY

(Erase heading not required.)

152nd M.G. Coy

Place	Date	Hour	Summary of Events and Information	Remarks and references to Appendices
HEDAUVILLE	30.12.16		Moved to huts in W.11.C. to huts by 11.45 am.	M.D.
MARTINSART	31.12.16		In billets. Fatigues.	M.D.

W Douglas Capt
O.C. 152 M.G. Coy

Confidential

Vol 8

122nd Machine Gun Company

War Diary for January 1917

Volume VIII

Army Form C. 2118.

WAR DIARY
or
INTELLIGENCE SUMMARY
(Erase heading not required.)

Volume VIII

182nd M.G. Coy.

Place	Date	Hour	Summary of Events and Information	Remarks and references to Appendices
MARTINSART	1.1.17		In Support. Fatigues.	nil
do	2		do	nil
do	3		do	nil
do	4		do	nil
do	5		do	nil
do	6		Moved in to line to relieve No 183 M.G. Coy. 14 guns in line and 2 guns of teams at Coy Hqrs at MOUQUET FARM. Relief began at 4:0 p.m. and was completed at 6:30 p.m. without casualties. Enemy shelling was light except near THIEPVAL.	nil
MOUQUET FARM	7		Artillery rather active in RAVINE during the morning, nothing of interest to report.	nil
do	8		Day was exceptionally clear and nothing on both sides was active, though a stiff wind made aerial observation impracticable. One gun at R27.b.3½.8½ fired 3500 rounds indirect between hours of 8:0 p.m. and 2:0 a.m. at reverse slope of hill R10.c. via traversing 2° right, left. There was no retaliation.	nil

2449 Wt. W14957/M90 750,000 1/16 J.B.C. & A. Forms/C.2118/12.

Army Form C. 2118.

WAR DIARY
or
INTELLIGENCE SUMMARY
(Erase heading not required.)

Instructions regarding War Diaries and Intelligence Summaries are contained in F.S. Regs., Part II. and the Staff Manual respectively. Title Pages will be prepared in manuscript.

182nd M.G. Coy

Place	Date	Hour	Summary of Events and Information	Remarks and references to Appendices
MOUQUET FARM	9/11/17	8.0 am	At 8.0 am a 24 hour bombardment of enemy lines began. Day after opening with heavy shrapnel cleared up after 10.0 and observation was fair. Enemy retaliation now weak except occasionally on our own front line.	N.D.
do	10/11/17		Our bombardment was continued still during but little enemy retaliation. Observation was fair.	N.D.
do	11	6.37 am	Under cover of creeping barrage, platoons of 8th R.W.R. raided FOLLY trench throughout its length and 1 Coy 8th R.W.R. raided 250x GRANDCOURT TRENCH from R.16.b.4.8 to SIXTEEN ROAD inclusive. 6 of our guns co-operated by firing indirect on the wiring ground R11A where enemy M.G's were expected to come into action in the open. In case of break down a gun being put out of action 2 guns were held in reserve and laid on targets guides being sent with teams firing with instructions to open fire reserve guns in case of these guns being raided. Target Same as 2 (see note by) Same as 3 also.	N.D.

EMERGENCY GUNS

(7) R.22.C.4½.6
(8) R.22.C.3½.6½

WAR DIARY or INTELLIGENCE SUMMARY

Army Form C. 2118.

Place	Date	Hour	Summary of Events and Information	Remarks and references to Appendices
MOUQUET FARM	Jan 1917	contd.	182nd M.G. Coy(?)	

GUNS.
① R.23.b.4.3.
② R.22.b.7.3.
③ R.22.b.6.3.
④ R.22.b.3/2.5
⑤ R.22.A.6.7.
⑥ R.21.D.2/2.5

TARGETS.
Sunken road R.5.c.7/2.1. — R.11.a.9/2.
Wood R.11.A. 2/2. 2/2.
do. R.11.A. 3½. 1/2.
Traverse trench R.11.A.1/2.3. — R.11.A.6.6.
End of trench R.11.A.3½.4. traversing left & right
Traversing trench R.11.A.1/2.5. — R.2.b.6.7½.

Guns opened well, brought to bear and with barrage. One emergency gun was employed. Fire control was carried out by pistol ammunition giving misfire.

The morning was very foggy and formation was invisible.

Registration on left and light co-ordinated by lining on (a) BEAUCOURT — MIRAUMONT ROAD, (b) High ground P.2.D and R.3.C and (c) new trench R.11.A. 8/2.9 — R.11.G.3.0.

One of our guns was troubled by enemy retaliation which came our front line most heavily and troubled our 2nd line but little.

Screens were used & fire through.

h.O.

Army Form C. 2118.

WAR DIARY
or
INTELLIGENCE SUMMARY

(Erase heading not required.)

Instructions regarding War Diaries and Intelligence Summaries are contained in F. S. Regs., Part II. and the Staff Manual respectively. Title Pages will be prepared in manuscript.

132nd M.G. Coy

Place	Date Jan 1917	Hour	Summary of Events and Information	Remarks and references to Appendices
MOUQUET FARM	12	—	Observation fair and good at times. Artillery active on both sides. Nothing of interest to report.	A.D
	13	—	Day very quiet. Enemy shelled MEERUT at its junction with FIELD about midday.	A.D
	14	—	Misty during day. Enemy having a shield a scheme of ground about R27A very heavily during morning and afternoon.	A.D
	15	5-30 pm	Company relieved by 54 M.G.Coy. Relief attempted owing to heavy shell taking place about line. Relief complete about 11-30 p.m. On relief Coy marched to RUBEMPRÉ via huts Avre.	A.D
RUBEMPRÉ	16		Rested	A.D
do	17		Marched to GORGES	A.D
GORGES	18		Marched to CRAMONT	A.D
CRAMONT	19		Marched to FOREST L'ABBAYE	A.D
FOREST L'ABBAYE	20		Cleaning	A.D

Army Form C. 2118.

WAR DIARY
or
INTELLIGENCE SUMMARY

(Erase heading not required.)

Instructions regarding War Diaries and Intelligence Summaries are contained in F. S. Regs., Part II. and the Staff Manual respectively. Title Pages will be prepared in manuscript.

182nd M.G. Coy.

Place	Date	Hour	Summary of Events and Information	Remarks and references to Appendices
FOREST L'ABBAYE	21		Shearing	hd
do	22			hd
do	23		Company Training	hd
do	24		do	hd
do	25		do	hd
do	26		do	hd
do	27		do	hd
do	28		do	hd
do	29		do	hd
do	30		do	hd
do	31		do	hd

h. Douglas Capt.
O.C. 182nd M.G. Coy.

182 M G Coy
Vol 9

182 MGC
WAR DIARY
FEBRUARY 1917.

VOLUME Nº IX

Army Form C. 2118.

WAR DIARY
or
INTELLIGENCE SUMMARY
(Erase heading not required.)

Volume IX

182nd M.G. Coy.

Place	Date	Hour	Summary of Events and Information	Remarks and references to Appendices
FOREST L'ABBAYE	FEBRUARY 1		Company Training	W.D
	2		do	W.D
	3		do	W.D
	4		do	W.D
	5		Marched to ST FIRMIN	W.D
ST FIRMIN	6		Practised on 400x range at LE BOUT DES CROCS	W.D
	7		do	W.D
	8		do	W.D
	9		Demonstrations etc on Lewis & Indirect fire etc.	W.D
	10		Marched to HAUTVILLERS	W.D
HAUTVILLERS	11		Rejoined Brigade at BELLANCOURT	W.D
BELLANCOURT	12		Company Training	W.D
	13		do	W.D
	14		do	W.D
	15		Entrained at PONT REMY for MARCELCAVE. Detrained at MARCELCAVE and marched to AUBERCOURT.	W.D
AUBERCOURT	16		Company Training	W.D
	17		do	W.D
	18		do	W.D
	19		Marched to VAUVILLERS. Bde in Reserve.	W.D

Army Form C. 2118.

WAR DIARY
or
INTELLIGENCE SUMMARY

(Erase heading not required.)

182nd M.G. Coy.

Place	Date Feby.	Hour	Summary of Events and Information	Remarks and references to Appendices
VAUVILLERS	20		Company training	h.O
do	21		do	h.O
do	22		do	h.O
do	23		do	
do	24		do	
do	25	4.0 a.m	Company relieved 183 M.G. Coy in the KRITZ sector. 12 guns in the line and 4 in reserve. There were no special incidents during the day. All quiet generally. Enemy artillery was the usual the usual 1 the enemy the minenwerfers. Occasionally shelled by the Brigade front line area and grouping troops and in front. Bombardment by howitzers and trench mortar batteries at dusk in rear of line.	h.O
VERMANDOVILLERS	26		Observation was excellent and hostile artillery was quiet. Enemy approached trenches walking boldly in our line. Howitzers were actively hostile and a counter-battery work and observation on our lines	h.O
	27		Weather was fine and observation fair. Moved to new headquarters not disturbed for	h.O
	28	10.2.10 a.m	2 Lewis was relieved at the line by the No.1 Coy. & moved to our billets at Vermandovillers	h.O

R. W. Johnson Capt.
O.C. 182 M.G. Coy.

Vol 10

182 Machine Gun Coy.

War Diary for March 1914/-

Volume X

Army Form C. 2118.

WAR DIARY
or
INTELLIGENCE SUMMARY
(Erase heading not required.)

Vol 3. 182nd M.G. Coy

Instructions regarding War Diaries and Intelligence Summaries are contained in F. S. Regs., Part II. and the Staff Manual respectively. Title Pages will be prepared in manuscript.

Place	Date MARCH	Hour	Summary of Events and Information	Remarks and references to Appendices
VERMAND-OVILLERS	1		Enemy artillery was quiet during day but was active at night. Our artillery sent flares over enemy lines during the afternoon of anomaly.	A.D.
	2		Enemy active, keep it down. Enemy active up again, front. Our artillery arrived prompt, fired a at Germans.	A.D.
	3		Artillery quiet on both sides. A small party of Huns was fired on by L.G. without result. Enemy reported to be alert.	A.D.
	4		German Salient S.39 was registered in morning by 4.5" & 6" Hows. Observation particularly good in morning when the salient was bombarded. Enemy retaliation was slight.	A.D.
	5		Day quiet. Enemy shelled track on and with 4.2" & 5.9". Enemy M.G.'s active at night. Several German Aeroplanes passed over our lines during afternoon.	A.D.
	6		Visibility was very good. ABLAINCOURT was shelled in the early morning. At 6.15 am L.T.M.'s carried out a small shoot.	A.D.

Army Form C. 2118.

WAR DIARY
or
INTELLIGENCE SUMMARY
(Erase heading not required.)

Instructions regarding War Diaries and Intelligence Summaries are contained in F. S. Regs., Part II. and the Staff Manual respectively. Title Pages will be prepared in manuscript.

182nd M.G. Coy.

Place	Date	Hour	Summary of Events and Information	Remarks and references to Appendices
VERMANDOVILLERS.	7		Artillery rather more active ABLAINCOURT shelled at intervals during day	h/d
	8		L.T.M's again carried out a small shoot. Hostile guns retired by 184 M.G. Coy.	
			Very quiet during day. At 6.6 p.m. Coy was relieved by 183 M.G. Coy.	
			Relief complete by 10.0 p.m. Coy proceeded to billets at HARBONNIERES.	h/d
HARBONNIERES	9		Company bathed & refitted.	h/d
	10		Kit Inspection — cleaning of material. etc.	h/d
	11		Company Training	h/d
	12		do	
	13		do	
	14		Company relieved 184 M.G. Coy in the ABLAINCOURT Sector. Guides met at 7.15 p.m. Relief complete 5.30 a.m 15th. Several guides were temporarily "lost".	h/d
DENIECOURT	15		Enemy Artillery quiet — a few 4.65 hers distributed in ELEPHANT TRENCH about midnight. Enemy snipers busy in right battalion front.	J.G.

WAR DIARY
or
INTELLIGENCE SUMMARY
(Erase heading not required.)

Army Form C. 2118.

Place	Date	Hour	Summary of Events and Information	Remarks and references to Appendices
DENIÉCOURT	16.		Enemy artillery fairly active during day. Enemy aeroplanes flying low over ELEPHANT TRENCH — ABLAINCOURT and NAMELESS FARM. Enemy M.G's searched between T.8.D.8.7 & T.8.D.25.5. during night. R.E. were also very busy against aircraft during day.	1/82 Machine Gun Coy. 4/9/S
— do — ASSEVILLERS	17.		Enemy aircraft very active during day. Artillery fire much below normal.	4/9/S
ABLAINCOURT	18		Guns reported that enemy had vacated his front three lines of trenches. Company was ordered to move H.Q's to ABLAINCOURT. Eight machine guns took also four battalions which up to this time, and running from T.21.A.6.9½. 16. T.26.B.3.4. Eight remaining guns were kept with support battalion at ABLAINCOURT.	4/9/S
MARCHELEPOT	19.		(6) H.Q's established at MARCHELEPOT. Eight guns advanced with two Front battalions 18.2/6 & 21/9 R.D.R. & took up positions in support company on line running between MORCHAIN & LICOURT. Eight advance guns advanced forward with Support battalion 2/1 R.W.R. to MARCHELEPOT. No Sign of enemy during day or night. Jumpoff board for MAINCOURT to DENIÉCOURT.	V.D.C.
— do —	20		Four guns placed in LIGOURT following village. Three guns en Erie, hurrying from C.7. C.N.6. K.C.13. B.0.15. one gun was left in reserve at section 3½. D.6. Eight nearest teams advanced eight against enemy leaving in forward positions.	4/9/S

WAR DIARY or INTELLIGENCE SUMMARY

Army Form C. 2118.

13/2 Machine Gun Coy

Place	Date	Hour	Summary of Events and Information	Remarks and references to Appendices
MARCHELEPOT	22/3/17		Eight forward guns moved up to SOMME CANAL. Four guns (placed) in EPENANCOURT protecting bridge head, which was under repair, a protective hillage, two gun placed in FALVY working in conjunction with lewis guns – Two (guns) (there) in PARGNY protecting bridge (which was badly damaged) two M.G. gun placed with which to cross water. Coy H.Qrs. & Coy reserve guns as before.	Y.J.R.
-do-	23rd		Situation unchanged – work done by forward teams on gun emplacements	Y.J.R.
-do-	24th		Situation unchanged – reserve gun team were road making under Brigade orders from 9AM to 4PM.	Y.J.R.
-do-	25th		Situation unchanged – reserve gun teams mending roads from 9AM to 3.30PM. Work at emplacements carried on by forward teams.	Y.J.R.
PARGNY	26th		Coy H.Qrs & eight reserve guns moved to PARGNY – transport etc. moved here from DENIECOURT. Forward gun positions unchanged. Great difficulty was experienced in moving D.M. Stores as four limbers were taken by Brigade for fatigue work.	Y.J.R.

WAR DIARY or INTELLIGENCE SUMMARY

Army Form C. 2118.

160 Machine Gun Co.

Place	Date	Hour	Summary of Events and Information	Remarks and references to Appendices
DEVISE	27		Coy. H. Qrs. & two sections left PARGNY at 6.30 PM & arrived at DEVISE at 11.45 PM where they billeted for night. One section moved from previous position to MERAUCOURT - MONTECOURT	
TERTRY	28		Coy. H. Qrs & two sections moved to TERTRY at 8.30 PM. No 3 section took up position in 1/8 Borderricks on left position front at Q.22.C.7.8 - Q.23.C.7.6 - Q.22.D.7.3 & Q.29.A.4.3. No 2 section took up position with 1/7 Warwicks on right with both sections at Q.29.C.3.5 - Q.35.A.1.4 - Q.35.C.3.6.4 on line in advance of Q.35.D.7.2. Situation unchanged. Three teams in the morning patrolled the lines. There was no actual attack on the enemy's. It was impossible to have observation during day as enemy artillery was active. Enemy reported holding Blue SOYECOURT - VERMAND. One Gun from No 2 section (Reserve) sent forward as an infantry patrol to SAILORS WOOD to pick up the party in attack on SOYECOURT & 1/8 Warwicks - the attack was postponed till 1 am. Remained in position.	

WAR DIARY
or
INTELLIGENCE SUMMARY.
(Erase heading not required.)

Army Form C. 2118.

Place	Date	Hour	Summary of Events and Information	Remarks and references to Appendices
DEVISE	30th		Orders for attack on SOYECOURT received. Reconnaissance was found impossible from Devise & places at disposal of Gen. Harmsworth who was taken for Gen. Fabrys from the attack on M/gun ahead in SAILORS WOOD was at suicide. The CO of Roswicks (the Bn Comr. Rd.) was large position at all. The Bn came under M/gun fire on leaving trench (own) at 6.00am before reserve company & reaching her final in SOYECOURT which had been taken with little opposition. There were no casualties in the Company. Coy 3 M/G & remaining gun teams moved back to DEVISE during the afternoon. Positions 2 guns in SOYECOURT & in left but No. 1 in large ( ). 1 gun in M/G Battery by Colonel in DEVISE right. Shelling of PT SQUEAK by the enemy in SOYECOURT drove gun teams of remaining guns moving back with Infantry. Cavalry held at top part of village some guns	No Machine Gun Coy 4/4
" "	31st			4/4

Confidential

Vol XI

No 182 M.G. Coy.

War Diary.

1st April 1917 to 30th April 1917

(Volume 11)

(Volume 11)

WAR DIARY
or
INTELLIGENCE SUMMARY.
(Erase heading not required.)

Army Form C. 2118.

Place	Date	Hour	Summary of Events and Information	Remarks and references to Appendices
DÉVISE	April 1st		16th hacking fire (?) relieved section in SOYÉCOURT at 11:0 A.M. Section received to withdraw and section also to be on left bank from to DÉVISE. Coy established in Barns & dugouts in DÉVISE. Company & first line transport moved to billets in NÉRAUCOURT.	For Actions see Appx 1 J.G. J.G.
NÉRAUCOURT	2nd			J.G.
-do-	3rd		Company formed working party, worked on crater in MANCHY LAGACHE from 9.0 A.M to 3.30 P.M.	J.G.
-do-	4th		Working party as before 6.0 A.M to 12.30 P.M. No 1 & 4. Sections (?moved) to TREFCON to support 163 M.G. Coy.	J.G.
-do-	5th		No 2 & 8 Sections worked in billets & surrounding NOITY Sections supported an attack on FRESNOY LE PETIT. The 300 yards (?) per firm into this village before infantry advanced. No 2&3 section returned to TREFCON after firing.	J.G.
-do-	6th		No work done by Company - No 1st & sections of coy supported an attack on FRESNOY LE PETIT - They returned to billets in VILLEVÊQUE.	J.G.

WAR DIARY or INTELLIGENCE SUMMARY

Army Form C. 2118.

183 Machine Gun Coy.

Place	Date	Hour	Summary of Events and Information	Remarks and references to Appendices
VILLEVEQUE	7.4.17		Company moved to VILLEVEQUE & took over lines from 163 M.G. Coy. Coy HQrs established at VILLEVEQUE – Q.M. Stores – remainder of Transport stayed at TREFCON. No 2 & 3 Sections relieved 8 guns of 163 M.G. Coy in following positions. N.32.c.8.6. M.32 B.17. M.25.B.82. N.25.B.3.6. R.24.A.6.4 – R.16.c.7.1 – R.18.c.6.3 – R.17.c.8.4. Relief completed by 12.0 midnight. Enemy artillery active – no casualties.	M.G.
–do–	8.4.17	7.0 pm	Our artillery cut wire preparatory in preparation for attack on FRESNOY – LE PETIT and Hill 120. After 40 minutes preparation by artillery 2/7 WARWICKS attacked & after stiff opposition took FRESNOY. 2 M.G.'s fired during attack	hd.
do	9.4.17	4.55 pm 5.15 am	on to FAYET – TRESNOY ROAD. 2 Vickers guns were placed at M.27.b.9.2, M.27.d.4.8 to enfilade an ALBATROSS aeroplane brought down the previous evening at VILLEVEQUE by French aviators. 2/6 WARWICKS took without opposition the French system running from HILL 120. 2 M.G.'s were pushed into the trench immediately later. Patrols sent to BERTHAUCOURT were fired on.	hd.
do	10-4-17	5.45	Enemy attacked TRESNOY with about 30 men who were also forced by L.G.'s. Our artillery was active – enemy inactive – except by inclined to gas at FRESNOY.	hd.

Army Form C. 2118.

WAR DIARY
or
INTELLIGENCE SUMMARY.
(Erase heading not required.)

Instructions regarding War Diaries and Intelligence Summaries are contained in F. S. Regs., Part II. and the Staff Manual respectively. Title pages will be prepared in manuscript.

182 MACHINE GUN COY

Place	Date	Hour	Summary of Events and Information	Remarks and references to Appendices
	APRIL 1917			
VILLEVEQUE	11		Day quiet.	nil
"	12	7.0 pm	Company relieved by No 10th M.G. Coy	nil
"		3.0 am	Relief complete. Company on relief marched to QUIVIERES to rest billets	nil
QUIVIERES	13		Cleaning	nil
"	14		Fatigues	nil
"	15		Fatigues	nil
"	16		Company Training	nil
"	17		Fatigues	nil
"	18		Fatigues	nil
"	19		Preparation for tour in line	
"	20		Company marched from QUIVIERES to SAVY (9 miles) and relieved 14 M.G. Coy in the line. 8 guns with Posts in the Outpost line and 8 guns in reserve in Quarry	
SAVY	21		about 5.21.b. (References are to Map 62 B S.W. Edition 2 A.) Movement of enemy near posts by day as all valleys coming towards ST QUENTIN. 2 guns in Quarry are provided with Anti Aircraft sights and kept mounted from dawn to dusk. Our positions everywhere dominated by the town of S⁺ QUENTIN – the Cathedral	

Army Form C. 2118.

WAR DIARY
or
INTELLIGENCE SUMMARY.
(Erase heading not required.)

182 M.G. Coy.

Instructions regarding War Diaries and Intelligence Summaries are contained in F.S. Regs., Part II. and the Staff Manual respectively. Title pages will be prepared in manuscript.

Place	Date	Hour	Summary of Events and Information	Remarks and references to Appendices
SAVY	APRIL 20		in particular supplying an excellent O.P. (moving steamer).	N.D.
"	21	5.0 am.	Relief complete 5.0 am. Enemy artillery very active – chiefly 4.2" & 5.9". Favourite enemy targets are SAVY WOOD, CEPY FARM, THE BLUFF, THE HALTE & areas S.17 a & b. A large fire started behind BARRACKS in ST QUENTIN and burned all night. Enemy aircraft active but flying too high to be taken on by M.G.s.	N.D.
"	22		Enemy artillery active again, especially during night, and about 20 enemy planes were over during day. Our artillery kept quiet during day, shelling intermittently during night. Our front posts were heavily shelled at intervals.	N.D.
"	23		Enemy artillery especially active during the morning and our batteries in S.14 & S.26d were shelled. M.G. position at S.12.A.5.5 was heavily shelled and the dugout and trench destroyed, gun was buried but no casualties. Enemy M.G. fired from CATHEDRAL Town during night.	N.D.
"	24		Enemy artillery active during day. Our artillery and the FRENCH replied effectively during night. Ox-gurdes? carried out on enemy positions, two being killed and 5 wounded. Great aerial activity, 15 being brought down over ST QUENTIN	

Army Form C. 2118.

WAR DIARY
or
INTELLIGENCE SUMMARY.
(Erase heading not required.)

Instructions regarding War Diaries and Intelligence Summaries are contained in F. S. Regs., Part II. and the Staff Manual respectively. Title pages will be prepared in manuscript.

182 M.G. Coy

Place	Date	Hour	Summary of Events and Information	Remarks and references to Appendices
SAVY	APRIL 24		Our planes were in evidence more than during the last five days. Our German planes engaged a French Battleplane at a great height which succeeded in escaping	shd
	25		Two guns (S6D23 + S6D4055) were relieved by 184 M.G. Coy. New positions of A Sec were through S13.B.10. – S80.7.0 – S11.A.0.1. – S12.a.5.4. Our post at S12.a. was shelled but no damage was done to gun crews. Fires again burning in ST. QUENTIN but they seem to be prepared as it is impossible to discover turned buildings by breweries with glasses. Bostels Roses was heavily shelled and 4 O.R. were killed + 1 wounded. Gun and 2 numbers with it were without.	N.D.
	26		Enemy artillery fairly active – no movement drawing fire. Our planes active by day + night. Enemy planes brought down by Frenchplane about 16y45 gun at S12.Aq.6 relieved by 184 M.G. Coy. Company has now 5 guns with Outposts – 6 guns in Picquet Line (BROWN LINE) and 5 guns in reserve in quarries about S21.a.5.5.	
	27		Our A.A. guns brought down an Albatros at 9.25a.m. Our machines active during the evening, 3 enemy were seen climbing toward ST MARTINS CHURCH	N.D.

WAR DIARY
or
INTELLIGENCE SUMMARY.

(Erase heading not required.)

Army Form C. 2118.

Place	Date	Hour	Summary of Events and Information	Remarks and references to Appendices
			182 M.G. Coy	
SAVY	APRIL 27		At ST QUENTIN.	
	28		Enemy artillery quiet during day. Our M.Gs near Bois des Roses were shelled with 77 mm. Biplane seen on hostile aerodrome flying towards evening.	h.b.
			Fires were again observed in ST QUENTIN.	
	29		Enemy artillery very active against our Batteries. M.G at Sts 4&5 was shelled during the day. Aircraft again active on both sides. Fires still burning in ST QUENTIN — they seem to be fed by the enemy with some kind of inflammable substance.	h.b.
	30		Enemy artillery continued active throughout the day especially against SAVY WOOD. Our planes more active than the enemy's. At night our howitzers fired on Q BARRACKS.	h.b.

W.D.Douglascath
O.C. 182 M.G. Coy

Confidential

Vol 12

No 182 Machine Gun Company

War Diary

From 1st May 1917 to 31st May 1917

"Volume — 12"

Army Form C. 2118.

WAR DIARY
or
INTELLIGENCE SUMMARY.
(Erase heading not required.)

Instructions regarding War Diaries and Intelligence Summaries are contained in F. S. Regs., Part II. and the Staff Manual respectively. Title pages will be prepared in manuscript.

193rd M.G. Coy   Volume XII

Place	Date	Hour	Summary of Events and Information	Remarks and references to Appendices
SAVY	MAY 1		Enemy artillery rather inactive in spite of brilliant weather. Our M.G's fired on several hostile planes without result. The range being somewhat lower. A large fire was observed in the BARRACKS and appeared to be a gunner fire — and smoke from several observed in ST QUENTIN. Enemy M.G's were rather quiet during the night and early morning.	h.D.
	2		Enemy artillery showed increased activity and our Heavies fired on the Ramparts. Our M.G's fired several bursts at enemy planes — which were very active — but chiefly with the idea of frightening them, as they were flying high.	h.D.
	3		Both artilleries were quiet. Planes less active than usual. Enemy M.G's fired bursts throughout the night.	h.D.
	4		Our artillery more active than the enemy during day. Our M.G's again engaged hostile aircraft though without result. Enemy machines seem particularly active during the early hours of the morning.	h.D.
	5		Artillery on both sides quiet. Our AA guns brought down a G. 24 "B" plane during the afternoon though enemy planes were generally inactive	h.D.

Army Form C. 2118.

WAR DIARY
or
INTELLIGENCE SUMMARY.
(Erase heading not required.)

Summary of Events and Information 182nd M.G. Coy.

Place	Date	Hour	Summary of Events and Information	Remarks and references to Appendices
SAVY	MAY 6		Both artilleries quiet. Our planes much busier than the enemy's. Enemy M.G's - unusual - fired indiscriminately during the night.	h.S.
	7.		Our artillery rather more active than the German. Germans were observed on the Tower of the CATHEDRAL. Enemy planes were again noticeable active in the early morning.	h.S.
	8.		Hostile artillery quiet during day but more active after dark. Our artillery quiet. Enemy M.G. reported firing by night from CATHEDRAL.	h.S.
	9.		Enemy artillery rather more active, ours normal. German planes were inactive throughout the day while ours showed their normal activity. Enemy Machine Gunning very active at night.	h.S.
	10		Enemy artillery normal. Our Artillery carried out a slow bombardment of the Enemy lines, the French Artillery co-operating. A fair number of Boche Machines (aeroplanes) were seen.	QQB3
	11		Our artillery was fairly quiet during the day. Enemy artillery unusually active during the morning. Enemy aeroplanes active. Our M.G's fired on enemy aircraft on several occasions during the day, our LEWIS Guns also fired.	QQB

Army Form C. 2118.

WAR DIARY
or
INTELLIGENCE SUMMARY.
(Erase heading not required.)

Instructions regarding War Diaries and Intelligence Summaries are contained in F. S. Regs., Part II. and the Staff Manual respectively. Title pages will be prepared in manuscript.

183rd M. E. COY.

Place	Date	Hour	Summary of Events and Information	Remarks and references to Appendices
SAVY	MAY. 12		Enemy artillery was active at times during the day & in the evening. Our Artillery during the day & night poured attention to the BARRACKS & the north west area of ST QUENTIN. Enemy aircraft was active. Fires were visible at night, one in ST QUENTIN & one in the direction of NEUVILLE ST AMAND.	
	13.		The Enemy artillery were inactive throughout the day. Ours was fairly active against the BARRACKS & defences about ROCOURT Salient. Aeroplanes of both sides were fairly active, & hostile AA guns were extremely quiet. Our M.Guns fired on enemy aeroplanes during the day. A large fire was observed in ST QUENTIN during the night.	
	14.		Enemy artillery quiet. Our Artillery of fresh between 6.0PM & 3.15AM. The Bgde M.G Coy was relieved by the French during the night. The 21st French Infantry Regt. taking over.	
GERMAINE & CURCHY	15		The Coy. on relief marched to GERMAINE & rested there till 4.15 PM when it marched to CURCHY.	
	16		The Coy. afternoon rested.	
OLINCOURT CHATEAU, FLESSELLES	17.		The Coy. was inspected by the Co. in the morning & entrained at NESLE at 4.40PM detraining at AILONGUEAU & marched to OLINCOURT CHAT. near FLESSELLES.	

Army Form C. 2118.

WAR DIARY
or
INTELLIGENCE SUMMARY.
(Erase heading not required.)

Instructions regarding War Diaries and Intelligence Summaries are contained in F. S. Regs., Part II. and the Staff Manual respectively. Title pages will be prepared in manuscript.

182 M.G. Coy

Place	Date	Hour	Summary of Events and Information	Remarks and references to Appendices
OLINCOURT	18		The Coy rested	
	19		Company training Maths	
	20		Company training & Presentation of Ribbons & Church Parade.	
LONGUEVILLETTE	21		The Company marched to LONGUEVILLETTE	
	22		The Company was inspected by the Brigadier. Coy training preparing to move.	
IVERGNY	23		The Company marched to IVERGNY	
	24		The Company travelled by motor lorries to LE BAC du SUD & marched to BERNEVILLE	
BERNEVILLE	25		The Coy rested	
	26		Company training, Inspection by Brigadier & Baths	
	27		Company training	
	28		do. Capt. E W DANN resumed command of the Company	
	29		Company training.	
	30		Company training.	
	31		Private attack scheme, followed by service in Church other ranks through last firebr.	

W Dann Capt.
Cmdg. 182 Machine Gun Coy.

Confidential

Vol 13

=No. 182 Machine Gun Coy=

War Diary

June 1st 1917 to June 30th 1917

(Volume 13.)

Army Form C. 2118.

WAR DIARY
INTELLIGENCE SUMMARY
(Erase heading not required.)

182 Machine Gun Coy. VOLUME XII

Place	Date	Hour	Summary of Events and Information	Remarks and references to Appendices
ARRAS	June 1.	10 am	The Company left BERNEVILLE & marched into billets in RACE HOUSE LANGART, HQ & B Company	App B.
		4.30 pm	RUE DU PUITS ST 6552. Officers' Mess RUE DES CAPUCINS.	App B.
	2.		Coy. training + cleanup of billets, billets, billets in a very bad state. Enemy aircraft 11.30 pm.	App B.
	3.		Church parade 9.35 am. Area Orders hostile 1c-in (?) naval gun. Enemy gun range 10.30 pm	App B.
	4.		Coy. training in G.35 (France 57B).	App B.
	5.		" "	App B.
	6.		" " Transport lines. Also 200 + range in Queen Moat	App B.
	7.		" " G.35. Range.	
	8.		" "	
	9.		Lieut. returned with Sarcour's bugle cap arrivers. Lt. B.H. returns to hq from course at M.G. Base School, CAMIERS	App B.
	10.		Church Parade 9.30 am Section 2 takes over anti-aircraft protection of FAUBOURG of F dump on DAINVILLE ROAD. Relief complete 10 am.	App B.
	11.		The Company went to DAINVILLE leaving ARRAS 5.30 am. Section takes over anti-aircraft protection of dump n.e. of WARLUS.	App B.
DAINVILLE	12.		Two hostile aeroplanes made for F dump at 9 am. Both were brought down just	App B.

WAR DIARY or INTELLIGENCE SUMMARY.

(Erase heading not required.)

Army Form C. 2118.

Instructions regarding War Diaries and Intelligence Summaries are contained in F.S. Regs., Part II. and the Staff Manual respectively. Title pages will be prepared in manuscript.

Place	Date	Hour	Summary of Events and Information	Remarks and references to Appendices
DAINVILLE	June 12		Battle Areas. The hot line. Gun Officer Co.s fires 300 rounds. The Brigadier-General Commanding inspected the Company in wheeling order, less transport, at 2.45 p.m.	[sig]
	13		Company training – 25 yards range.	
			Company training	[sig]
	14		Company training	[sig]
	15		Lt. F. J. Goode returned from course to Hd. qrs. of Second in Command. Relief of No. 2 Section by No. 4 Section at Fosseaux dumps.	
			Relief of one subsection of No. 3 Section by the other, under 2/Lt W. Batham, at Marais camp.	
	16		Company training	[sig]
			Lectures. Musical Band at 7.30.	[sig]
	17		Company training	[sig]
	18		Musketry. Lyngdale lane Shoot.	[sig]
	19		Company Training	[sig]
	20		Company Training. Relief of teams at dumps cancelled.	[sig]
	21		Company training. Teams at dumps relieved by Coys from same from 12th Division.	[sig]
	22		Company training. Teams at dumps relieved by Lewis (Nashs) not [cut off]	

WAR DIARY or INTELLIGENCE SUMMARY.

Army Form C. 2118.

Place	Date	Hour	Summary of Events and Information	Remarks and references to Appendices
	June			
DRANOUTRE	22 (continued)		58th Division (7 & Fauquissart). The Batta relief was very much delayed because the incoming officers was only guided to points 2 hours instead of it. The Rgt. Bazars's losses by shell fire & rifle were 10 wounded, 3 amp of heavy trench	[B]
	23.		a Sgt for the R.O.S. completed by 23 p.m.	[B] [B]
WATOU			No. 1 Company at O.S.	[B] [B]
			Company Training.	[B] [B]
			Lewis gun Training.	[B] [B]
			Company Training. Bath.	[B] [B]
	24		Company Training.	[B]
	25		Company Training.	[B]
	26		Company Training. 685 S.S. Course.	[B]
	27		Company Training.	
	28			
	29			
	30			

Brown Capt.
O.C. 182 Machine Gun Coy

Confidential

Vol 14

War Diary
of
No 182 Machine Gun Coy.

July 1st to July 31st

(Volume 14)

WAR DIARY

INTELLIGENCE SUMMARY.

(Erase heading not required.)

Army Form C. 2118.

Summary of Events and Information 182 M.G. Coy. VOLUME XIV.

Place	Date	Hour	Summary of Events and Information	Remarks and references to Appendices
W.P.L	JULY			
	1		The Company rested.	A.B.
	2		Company Training.	A.B.
	3		Company Training.	A.B.
	4		Company Training. Indirect competitions.	A.B.
	5		Company Training. Competition finals by teams. Technical competitions.	A.B.
	6		Company Training. Competition finals les 4 a.m.	A.B.
	7		Company Training. Range.	A.B.
	8		Company Training. 2 section bombing course.	A.B.
	9		Brigade Church Parade & finals of competitions.	A.B.
	10		Company Training. 2 section bombing course.	A.B.
	11		Brigade holiday for Divisional Sports.	A.B.
	12		Company Training.	A.B.
	13		Company Training.	A.B.
	14		Company Training. Lt. J. Hunter left for U.K. re commission in Infantry.	A.B.
	15		No Company rested. 2/Lt. F.H. Poole joines the Coy. from M.G. Base.	A.B.
	16		Company Training. Indirect fire Scheme.	A.B.

WAR DIARY
or
INTELLIGENCE SUMMARY.

Army Form C. 2118.

Place	Date	Hour	Summary of Events and Information	Remarks and references to Appendices
	JULY			
WAIL	17		Company Training.	
	18		Company Training.	
	19		Company Training. Inoculations.	
	20		Company Training. Inoculations.	
	21		Company Training.	
	22		The Company rested.	
	23	9.15 am	The Bt.C. inspected the Company.	
	24	7.5 am	The Company marched by road 5 via PRÉVENT to	
BIBBEVILLE			BIBBEVILLE, billets there for the night.	
RUBROUCK AREA	25	10.30 pm	The Company entrained for BAVINCHOVE reaching there at 2.15 am.	
	26	11 am	The Company then us by road to RUBROUCK, arriving at 7.10 am, & went into billets.	
	27		The Bt.C. explained to C.O's conference the rôle & work in the supporting forward Company.	
			Training was carried on.	
	28		Company Training.	
	29		The Company rested.	
	30		Company Training.	
	31		Company Training.	

COMMANDING No 182 M.G. COY
31 July 1917

CONFIDENTIAL.

War Diary

Nº 182 Machine Gun Coy

From 1st Aug. 1917 to 31st Aug 1917

(Volume 15)

Army Form C. 2118.

WAR DIARY
or
INTELLIGENCE SUMMARY.
(Erase heading not required.)

182 M.G. Coy. VOLUME XV.

Instructions regarding War Diaries and Intelligence Summaries are contained in F. S. Regs., Part II. and the Staff Manual respectively. Title pages will be prepared in manuscript.

Place	Date	Hour	Summary of Events and Information	Remarks and references to Appendices
RUDBOUCK	Aug/67			
	1		Company Training.	A.B.
	2		Company Training.	A.B.
	3		Company Training.	A.B.
	4		Company Training.	A.B.
	5		No Company Training.	A.B.
	6		Brigade Trench attack. Corps Commander present.	A.B.
	7		Brigade Trench attack. Corps Commander present.	A.B.
	8		Brigade Trench attack. Corps Commander present. Lecture on MOPS battle by Brig. Gen. Bosher	A.B.
	9		Brigade Trench attack. Corps Commander present.	A.B.
	10		Company Training. 32 men from 182 Inf Bde attached to the Coy. as ammunition carriers & Rifle places left	A.B.
	11		Company Training	A.B.
	12		No Company Rested	A.B.
	13		Company Training.	A.B.
	14		Company Training.	A.B.
	15		Company Training.	A.B.
BRANDHOEK No. 1 AREA	16		The Division moved into XIX Corps area. The Coy. went into Hutments Buttown	A.B.

Army Form C. 2118.

WAR DIARY
or
INTELLIGENCE SUMMARY.
(Erase heading not required.)

Instructions regarding War Diaries and Intelligence Summaries are contained in F. S. Regs., Part II. and the Staff Manual respectively. Title pages will be prepared in manuscript.

Place	Date	Hour	Summary of Events and Information	Remarks and references to Appendices
BRANDHOEK	Aug OST			
AREA No. 1.			POTYZE/RYNGHE & VLAMERTINGHE.	
	17		8 guns were sent up to take the offensive barrages from part of XXXI Division, the situation being very confused. The new places in position with our left cavalry, one EA passed over at 10.15. 15 dropped about our O.P. Transport movement. The Boy) seems without incident.	[sgd]
	18			[sgd]
	19		Preparations now begun for MG barrage scheme for impending attack by 184 Bde. All officers visited the line. Two OPs.B. Gave Dr. Formless charge. Two batteries of 8 Guns. Lt. E.C.R Bain was detailed to communs that on the kept at 15. P.E. KER that on the left. Osman & Nolan both slightly wounded. Considerable enemy aerial activity tonight. Also H.V. shelling.	[sgd]
	20		Platforms prepared & guns in for barrage fire and 5 sent up straight to Lt. W.H. Tunner guns for barrage arrived from QMOS. Calculations checked. Two officer EA over straight & many bombs dropped. Much HV shelling, Sgt	
	21		Guns taken up to 5, signals, and two further communication tacks positions & barrage fire Lt. E.C.R BAIN in right batter group, Lt. REKER left battery group. CAPT E.W JANN	[sgd]

WAR DIARY
INTELLIGENCE SUMMARY

Army Form C. 2118.

Place	Date	Hour	Summary of Events and Information	Remarks and references to Appendices
BRANDHOEK No 1 CAMP	AUGUST 21		Coy Commenced 20 guns. Another 20 under Capt KERR, P.S. M.G. Coy, further forward, the Whole controlled by the D.A.D.O. Major W.R. ANDERSON. Headrs. Company not actually holding any of guns, left behind at BRANDHOEK No.1.	(sd)
PREZENBERG D.20.c.d.3.c.4.7	22	4.45am	At Zero all gun teams were ready, in spite of a very heavy all-night bombardment by enemy artillery, 10 guns in front of BOSSAERT Fm. & 10 guns behind CARNATION Fm., controlled from C.23.c.4.7. Directly our artillery & m.g. barrage began the enemy put down a series of barrages, the nearmost of which was very near our m.g. emplacements & caused 3 casualties (all wounded). Guns continued for 10 minutes on main WINNIPEG - GALLIPOLI Pm, for 40 minutes on a line WURST Fm. - FOKKER Fm. The guns were then withdrawn and the Coy. made its way back to camp at BRANDHOEK 1, after a great ordeal by war.	(sd)
BRANDHOEK 1	23		The Company cleaned up guns, & and rested. No B.G.C. visits the Coy. lines & watches the men for their work of the day before. Orders were received from LXI Division for the Company, as infantryman of the Brigade, to move into the line on the night of the 24th. Dispositions :—	

Army Form C. 2118.

WAR DIARY
or
INTELLIGENCE SUMMARY.
(Erase heading not required.)

Place	Date	Hour	Summary of Events and Information	Remarks and references to Appendices
	Aug.			
BRANDHOEK No 1	23		2 Guns Section 2 at SOMME Fm. 2 Guns Section 2 at DON'T TRENCH. Section 4 at JEW HILL. Section 3 at BANK FARM. Section 1 at CAPRICORN TRENCH right of WIELTJE - SPREE Fm road.	A.B.
WIELTJE SECTOR	24		Relay went into the line the night of 24/25. The CAPRICORN TRENCH line was heavily shelled during the night, and one gun was knocked out by a direct hit. Two men were wounded. These guns were ordered for protective barrage.	
	25		The following instructions received from Division. 6 Guns renew SOMME - POND Fm. — DON'T TRENCH. 8 Guns at disposal of 183 Inf. Bde. (CAPRICORN TRENCH). 2 Guns JEW HILL. The guns in CAPRICORN TRENCH were subjected to several hours' shelling from HE 5mm heavies, but no casualties were sustained.	A.B.
	26		Dispositions were allied by(?) Division. Less objectives line GARRISON (inclusive) – B Central – SCHULER Fm. (inclusive) - WINNIPEG. 4 Guns 182 JEW HILL. 8 Guns 183 in CAPRICORN TRENCH. 2 Guns (P? POND) Fm., 2 in DON'T TRENCH – 2 in SOMME Fm. A word about D.13.C.80.05 to cover advance and also to act as defensive guns. Line of fire towards HURST Fm. - AVIATIK Fm. and upslopes towards FOKKER - MARTHA Redoubt. 2 Guns under G.O.C. 183 Inf. Bde. Zero fixed for 2 pm. 27th. An Enemy position were increasingly heavily shelled at intervals during the	

WAR DIARY or INTELLIGENCE SUMMARY

Army Form C. 2118.

Place	Date	Hour	Summary of Events and Information	Remarks and references to Appendices
WIKTJIE Sector	Aug. 26	day/night	O.C. 162 M.G. Coy. now has his H.Q. at POND FM.	2.1.9.
	27		established night of 26/27. Honorary patrol his orders were 8 guns 183 in CAPRICORN TRENCH, 2 at POND FM., 2 as B'de. reserve for consolidation in CAPRICORN TRENCH, 4 at JEW HILL, 4 A forward of CAPRICORN TRENCH, 1 at DONT-SOMME line. The infantry to take attack were in BELLEVUE in advance of POND FM line all night of 26/27 until Zero. In the morning of 27th heavy rain fell, and the whole countryside was reduced to uncover. The forward JEW HILL & SOMMIT - DONT - SOMME trenches became unholdable. When the attack was launched at 1.55 p.m. the enemy put down very heavy barrage on all our machine gun positions at Wichels out 3 men. His artillery and lofty concentrated fire from the position but a good deal of firing was nevertheless carried out. A lot barrage was put up from CAPRICORN TRENCH, though 183 suffered some casualties there, of harassing fire was carried on from all positions except SOMMIT -	

WAR DIARY or INTELLIGENCE SUMMARY

Army Form C. 2118.

Place	Date	Hour	Summary of Events and Information	Remarks and references to Appendices
WIELTJE SECTOR	Aug. 27		DGMT. Where the trenches could be found was an effort, but it was definite to keep the guns there (there they stay). As yet we have no targets. The attack proved to be a complete failure, and the rest of the day was spent in collecting casualties and restoring periodical enemy bombardments. At [?] dusk our barrage began again. Lasted 2 hours, presumably on SOS call. The night was moderately quiet.	
	28		A.F.(?) urgent representations had been made as to the unserviceability of the forward guns. Orders were received from Division. Dispositions:— 4 guns still trail 4 about W guns of Hill 35. 2 Pounder Fm. 2 Somme. Remaining 4 "where you wish in dry places". More places in CAPRICORN TRENCH then withdrew to JAPPER FM. Company headquarters thus removed to WIELTJE, & there attentions were carried out. Half 193 M.G. Coy. was moved up to WIELTJE, the intention being for them to augment 183 M.G. Coy.; but as 183 found this impracticable owing to the dugouts to the dugout 2 men having known in the 4th British line, the Germans evacuated the position left 2 were being known killed, 12 wounded, A3 M.G. Coy., were withdrawn in the buttle [?] pire.	

WAR DIARY
or
INTELLIGENCE SUMMARY.

(Erase heading not required.)

Army Form C. 2118.

Place	Date	Hour	Summary of Events and Information	Remarks and references to Appendices
	Aug.			
WIELTJE SECTOR	28		Morning working.	
	29		Arrangements were made for 184 Coy. to relieve 182, & for 182 to take over the Camp at BRANDHOEK No.1 again. An order was received from Division, at 5 pm, to situate touch with "M.G. Officer at MILL COTT to try to fix up defences on right flank. POMMERN REDOUBT & HILL 35 commence to our area." This was not wholly understood, as part of HILL 35 was known to be in enemy hands; but the order was carried out and dispositions were handed over to 184 M.G. Company. Relief was complete at 10.15 pm. The Coy. was placed on a narrow gauge train, but owing to a block on the line had to make their way into camp on foot they could.	R.B. M.B. E.B.
BRANDHOEK No.1	30		The Company rested.	
	31		Inventories cleaned & deficiencies made up again as possible. Casualties were from Spoure to last constitues however, further. Casualties 1 Officer and 24 or. to report sick; 6 killed; 1 missing believed killed; 9 wounded & shell shock. The subaltern Officer and 24 or. to report sick.	R.B.

W.Warner Capt.
Machine Gun Company. 182

Confidential

Vol 16

No 182 Machine Gun Coy

War Diary

From Sept 1st 1917 to Sept 30th 1917

(Volume 16).

Army Form C. 2118.

WAR DIARY or INTELLIGENCE SUMMARY.

(Erase heading not required.)

182 Machine Gun Coy.   Volume XVI.

Place	Date	Hour	Summary of Events and Information	Remarks and references to Appendices
RUDRAVER No.1.	Sept. 1		Further clean-up & taking up & Efficiency. Company Training.	
	2		Osbos recruits for further work on the line in a few days. Company Training. Hostile aircraft very active all night. About two Groppes came over the lines. 9 Wels to be replaced. No casualties.	
	3		Company Training. My aircraft supplemented day.	
WIELTJE SECTOR.	4th		8 guns 182 Machine gun coy. relieved 8 guns of 184 M.G.Coy. at the following places:— 4 at TEN HILL. 2 at POND FARM. 1 at DON'T TRENCH. } Section 2. Sergt Johnson 1 at C.19.a.15.90. } Section 3. Lieut Turner.	
	5		O.C. 182 moved his forward headquarters to WIELTJE at 8 p.m. Relief was complete at 11 p.m. The night was unusually quiet and undisturbed. Arrangements were made by the B.H.Q.O. for the remainder of the day. To fire a barrage in connection with an attack	

Army Form C. 2118.

WAR DIARY
or
INTELLIGENCE SUMMARY.
(Erase heading not required.)

Place	Date	Hour	Summary of Events and Information	Remarks and references to Appendices
WIELTJE SECTOR.	5		On GALLIPOLI. 4 more guns going to TEN HILL and 2 to CAPRICORN TRENCH. This was however countermanded, the message arriving too late to prevent the men and guns moving to WIELTJE. They were sent back forthwith. 8 guns of 183 and the 8 of 182 M.G. Coy were put under O.O.182. A series of attacks who made by the Brigade on A15115. HOUSE and HILL 35. IBERIAN and BECK HOUSE were also attacked by the Division on the right. These strong points were bombarded by our heavy artillery with Armour-piercing shell, largely 9.2 mich. and many direct hits were observed. An S.O.S. went up at 9.30 and our machine guns and those of 183 M.G. Coy fired 18000 rounds during the night. 2 men of No 2 Section were killed and 1 wounded.	
	6		News came that IBERIAN and BECK HOUSE were in our hands but the situation remained obscure during the greater	

Army Form C. 2118.

WAR DIARY
or
INTELLIGENCE SUMMARY.
(Erase heading not required.)

Place	Date	Hour	Summary of Events and Information	Remarks and references to Appendices
WIELTJE SECTOR.	6		Rest of the day. A good deal of consolidation work was done by the Company.	
	7		No day was uneventful. The 2 guns + the Coy. Commander were relieved by 2 Guns 3/183 M.G. Coy and by Capt D.H. PECK, one casualty, Sergt JOHNSON being wounded, being sustained. The relief was greatly disturbed by barrage counter-barrage artillery work.	
	8		The Company cleaned up greatly. One man + a Runner was brought in. an S.A.A. party was sent to salvage Neuve, without success.	
	9		Company Training. The party was again sent + Pte BIRD was brought out without mishap. He had stuck to his cherged-ment carefully	
	10		The Company rested, it being Sunday, but salvaging Neuve, was resumed with extra fatigue Corps, was begun. This was previously necessary by	
	11		Great enemy aerial activity. Company training. Transports instructions.	
	12		Company training. Defences strengthened. 3 hrs anti-aircraft emplacements ready.	

WAR DIARY
or
INTELLIGENCE SUMMARY.
(Erase heading not required.)

Army Form C. 2118.

Place	Date	Hour	Summary of Events and Information	Remarks and references to Appendices
PRANDHOEK.	13		Company training.	
	14		The Company was lent to water no. 1 area.	
SEHOUDENHOEK.	15		Company training. Inspection of transport by the B.G.C.	
	16		Company rested.	
	17		The Company moved to EECKE AREA	
EECKE AREA	18		Company training	
	19		The Company entrained at CAESTRE station for ARRAS No. 1. arriving about 6 p.m.; after detraining the Company marched to billets in BERNEVILLE	
BERNEVILLE	20		Company training.	
	21		Company training. The Commanding Officer, 5 officers, + 1 Sergt, 1 L/Cpl + 1 N°1. visited the line = East of FAMPOUX.	(O.C. by on leave.)
	22		The Company left BERNEVILLE at 9.20 am and marched to ST. NICHOLAS AREA. (Billets in GRIMSBY CAMP).	
ST. NICHOLAS AREA	23		Company rested. 16 No. 1 went into the line E. of FAMPOUX.	

Army Form C. 2118.

WAR DIARY
or
INTELLIGENCE SUMMARY.
(Erase heading not required.)

Instructions regarding War Diaries and Intelligence Summaries are contained in F. S. Regs., Part II. and the Staff Manual respectively. Title pages will be prepared in manuscript.

Place	Date	Hour	Summary of Events and Information	Remarks and references to Appendices
ST NICHOLAS AREA	24	-	The Company moved into line E. of FAMPOUX 8 guns being in support line and 8 guns into firing line trenches	Y.J.G.
FAMPOUX	25.		Quiet day. Indirect fire was carried out on enemy tracks & communication trenches by guns in the reserve trenches	Y.J.G.
	26.		Our artillery very active firing on enemy front line & T.M. emplacements. Indirect fire carried on shelling back areas. Two enemy M.Gs. fired continuously during night on our communication & reserve trenches. Coy H. Qrs. at H.17.c.2.6. recieved attention from enemy 77 m.ms.	Y.J.G.
	27.		Day & night quiet. Occasional trench mortar shafts took place during the day. Enemy artillery more active, shelling our front line system & CHEMICAL WORKS. Indirect fire was carried out by four guns on enemy tracks. Our artillery replied actively to enemy T.Ms.	Y.J.G.

WAR DIARY
or
INTELLIGENCE SUMMARY.

(Erase heading not required.)

Army Form C. 2118.

Place	Date	Hour	Summary of Events and Information	Remarks and references to Appendices
FAMPOUX	28.9.17		Our heavy artillery shelled enemy back areas during day. 18 hrs. enfiladed enemy front line. Enemy artillery active during day, very quiet during night. One enemy plane was brought down over his lines by our machines — our aircraft were exceedingly active. Between 6.0 PM & 6.30 PM. eleven machines flying very low over enemy lines & firing into his trenches. Indirect fire was carried out during night.	JJG
	29.9.17		Our artillery carried out their usual harassing fire throughout the day. Enemy Artillery was more active than usual. Paying great attention to the CHEMICAL WORKS, and searching for our M.G. emplacements. Aeroplane activity on both sides was normal. Usual indirect fire was carried out on enemy tracks and communication trenches.	JJG
	30.9.17		At 1.0 am. the enemy commenced a heavy bombardment of our front system and back areas, lasting about 50 minutes. FAMPOUX received considerable attention a	JJG

WAR DIARY
or
INTELLIGENCE SUMMARY.

Army Form C. 2118.

Place	Date	Hour	Summary of Events and Information	Remarks and references to Appendices
FAMPOUX	30.9.17		Large number falling in the vicinity of Company Headquarters (H.7.c.2.b.) at 1.30 am. Gun S.O.S. was sent up. The Machine Guns immediately opened fire & it is believed with good results and our artillery put a barrage on "No mans land" and the enemy trenches were then heavily attempted to that forward on our left but was easily repulsed by M.G. fire. Hostile aeroplane activity was above normal. About 2 men two of our aeroplanes were brought down in flames behind our own lines. The remainder of the day passed without incident	J.G.

J.J. Crosby Lt
O.C. 180 M.G. Coy

CONFIDENTIAL

Vol 17

No 182 Machine Gun Coy

War Diary

From 1st October 1917 to 31st October 1917

(Volume — 17)

Army Form C. 2118.

WAR DIARY
or
INTELLIGENCE SUMMARY.

(Erase heading not required.)

Instructions regarding War Diaries and Intelligence Summaries are contained in F.S. Regs. Part II. and the Staff Manual respectively. Title pages will be prepared in manuscript.

Volume XVII

Place	Date	Hour	Summary of Events and Information	Remarks and references to Appendices
FAMPOUX	October			
	1		Normal indirect fire was carried out on enemy tracks & communication trenches between 4.30 pm & 4.50 am. 1200 rounds were expended. The enemy's machine gun were very active, but his usual CONTRA TRENCH & crew harassing fire strafing important parapets. Aircraft activity on both sides was below normal. 1 o.r. was wounded.	[s.d.]
	2		The usual indirect fire between 9.30pm & 4.30 am. 12,000 rounds expended. Aircraft activity - enemy's slight, our own normal. 1 o.r. was wounded slightly by enemy bullet. The enemy carried out a similar M.G. programme to that of last night.	[s.d.]
	3		Rain in the night turning first heavier, first part of morning, later, rain developed in the front of the Division on the night. Hutro consequences followed on our front. Our usual indirect fire programme was carried out between 9.30pm & 4.30 am. Our enemy tracks crossing the railways. 16,000 rounds expended. The enemy's indirect fire with machine guns was inconsiderable.	
	4		Artillery + T.m. work by the enemy was normal, and aerial activity was very slight. We expended 12,000 rounds on indirect fire.	[s.d.]
	5		Few aeroplanes were able to turn out until late afternoon. The day was quiet. A bombards shoot was arranged with M.5 howitzers and T.M.'s on enemy headquarters, followed a.m.	[s.d.]

2353 Wt W25141/1454 700,000 5/15 D.D. & L. A.D.S.S./Forms/C. 2118.

Army Form C. 2118.

WAR DIARY
or
INTELLIGENCE SUMMARY.
(Erase heading not required.)

Instructions regarding War Diaries and Intelligence Summaries are contained in F. S. Regs., Part II. and the Staff Manual respectively. Title pages will be prepared in manuscript.

Place	Date	Hour	Summary of Events and Information	Remarks and references to Appendices
FAMPOUX	6		The weather was bad, and aerial observation was difficult. Both sides however carried out a little aeroplane work. Enemy machine guns traversed our support lines and searched our O.P.'s occasionally. Our rifles were very active, & carried out a full programme of indirect fire.	AuB
	7		Another quiet day with intervals of bright weather. One of our MG emplacements, in COLOMBO, was knocked in by a salvo of small shells, but was successfully repaired and the trench cleared without casualty. Enemy machine - gunners moderately active. Our howitzers many targets as usual.	AuB
	8		Guns came for the re-fronting of all the guns in the sector, and on infantry part has details by Bde. to deepen + back-board camer TRENCH as a preliminary to digging accommodation for 8 Marrak's Guns.	AuB
	9		A quiet day. Enemy fancies tried to cross our lines, but were driven back by our AA, LG + MG. fire. 32,000 rounds were expended in indirect fire.	AuB
	10		Quiet day. 19,000 rounds expended at night. Emplacement in CORONA was finished to a certain extent by grantsworkers.	AuB
	11		Enemy aircraft were very active at 9 a.m., one flying very low over FAMPOUX. 24,000 rounds expended in indirect fire.	AuB

Army Form C. 2118.

WAR DIARY
or
INTELLIGENCE SUMMARY.
(Erase heading not required.)

Instructions regarding War Diaries and Intelligence Summaries are contained in F. S. Regs., Part II. and the Staff Manual respectively. Title pages will be prepared in manuscript.

Place	Date	Hour	Summary of Events and Information	Remarks and references to Appendices
FAMPOUX	12		Plans set in the early morning, & aerial activity was nil. 3000 rounds were expended on indirect fire on enemy tracks.	R/S
	13		The usual indirect fire programme was carried out at night. 1000 rounds were fired.	R/S
	14		A successful raid was carried out at 9.30pm by parties of the 2/5 Warwicks, 14 prisoners being taken & 30 other enemy killed. Our casualties nil. 8 guns of the company supported by firing 2000 rounds on enemy approaches to the raided area.	R/S
	15		The Coy. was relieved by 193 M.G. Coy & moved back to NEVIS BARRACKS, ARRAS. Everything went off smoothly.	R/S
ARRAS	16		Coy. training.	R/S
	17		Coy. training.	R/S
	18		Coy. training.	R/S
	19		Coy. training.	R/S
	20		Coy. training.	R/S
	21		Route march.	R/S
	22		Coy. training.	R/S

WAR DIARY
or
INTELLIGENCE SUMMARY.
(Erase heading not required.)

Army Form C. 2118.

Place	Date	Hour	Summary of Events and Information	Remarks and references to Appendices
ARRAS.	Oct. 22		Coy. training.	A.D.S.
	23		Coy. training.	A.D.S.
	24		Coy. training.	A.D.S.
	25		Coy. training.	A.D.S.
	26		Coy. training.	A.D.S.
	27		Preparations for relief.	A.D.S.
	28		The Coy. relieved 184 M.G. Coy. in the GREENLAND HILL Sector. Relief was complete by 12 noon. The night was quiet. 8000 rounds were fired from the barrage S.O.S. positions on enemy S.O.S.	A.D.S.
GREENLAND HILL SECTOR.	29		Enemy artillery was active on the CABIN P.T. during the day. 2000 rounds were expended in indirect fire. A raid took place in the FAMPOUX Sector, which was not successful as guns were strong.	A.D.S.
	30		The day was quiet the night normal. 2000 rounds were expended on indirect fire & enemy aircraft was heavily engaged without success.	A.D.S.
	31		There was a good deal of shelling on both sides and aircraft activity was great in the morning. 2000 rounds were expended in indirect fire. Four dugouts & tunnels were examined in conjunction with R.E.	A.D.S.

W. Davis Capt. Cmdg.
182 M.G. Company.

Vol 18

182 Machine Gun Company

War Diary

From 1st November 1917 to 30th November 1917

(Volume 18)

Confidential

Army Form C. 2118.

WAR DIARY
or
INTELLIGENCE SUMMARY.
(Erase heading not required.)

VOLUME XVIII.

Instructions regarding War Diaries and Intelligence Summaries are contained in F. S. Regs., Part II. and the Staff Manual respectively. Title pages will be prepared in manuscript.

Place	Date	Hour	Summary of Events and Information	Remarks and references to Appendices
GREENLAND HILL SECTOR.	NOV. 1		Enemy artillery shows an increase of activity, and our support line & C.T.'s become a good deal of attention. Our batteries fired 2500 rounds on enemy tracks. One signaller was wounded by an enemy bullet, other batteries poor shew.	
	2		Visibility was poor and aircraft were inactive. The enemy apparently struggles & rais on the front & the Division own left, but own reached our trenches. Hostile artillery has again active, on the same targets. Their batteries were apparently in action, & any activity shown met with a certain amount of retaliation. The night was fairly quiet.	
	3		The weather was very bright, and at no time was the visibility sun indicated. Gen. Batteries on both sides were fairly quiet until our 18pounders put a short practice barrage down upon the German front & support lines, which was replied to in the usual way. 18 Barrage guns in reserve relieved 8 support guns.	
	4		Our artillery was fairly active during the morning on enemy front and support lines. At 4.30pm our artillery co-operated with 47th Divisional Artillery in connection with a raid carried out by the 142nd Infy Bde. Enemy artillery was active during	

Army, Form C. 2118.

WAR DIARY
or
INTELLIGENCE SUMMARY.

(Erase heading not required.)

Place	Date	Hour	Summary of Events and Information	Remarks and references to Appendices
GREENLAND HILL SECTOR.	4		During the period and retaliated to our 4.20 pm bombardment. A few gas shells were also fired during the evening on our front system. Bearings taken on gun flashes from H.11.a.95.35 read 93°, 70°, 126°(T) at 4.48 pm this gun lifted on to our front-line from a barrage he had put down in "No Man's Land" 40 yards in front of our line. It covered chiefly of GRANATENWERFERS and 4.2". This kept up until 6 pm when he lifted on to CORK SUPPORT still continuing to fire GRANATENWERFERS on the front line which did not cease until about 8 pm. All was fairly quiet by 8.30 pm. Enemy T.M's were very active all day on CLAY ALLEY, CHARLIE SUPPORT. and COSTAR ALLEY. Our Machine Gun co-operated with the rough on our left - 2300 rounds being fired. No aerial (enemy) activity.	N.f.g.
	5		Our artillery throughout the day and night fires intermittently on enemy front and support lines. The activity of the enemy artillery was below normal	N.f.g.

Army Form C. 2118.

WAR DIARY
or
INTELLIGENCE SUMMARY.
(Erase heading not required.)

Place	Date	Hour	Summary of Events and Information	Remarks and references to Appendices
Greenland Hill Sector.	5		His T.M activity was much below normal, probably due to the amount of ammunition shot off on 4th inst. Our Machine Guns carried out indirect fire at Intervals during the night at the following targets:- (1) WEASEL and WILLOW. (2) I8.a.95. - I2.c.6.1. 3000 rounds were expended. Enemy M.Gs fired bursts at Intervals during the night sweeping our parapet and reaching our 6.Lt One or two bursts were also fired during the day. Enemy Aeroplanes actively below normal.	A.A.G.
	6		Throughout the day and night enemy artillery particularly at Quiet. Our artillery kept-up a harassing fire throughout the day and night. Our Machine Guns fired indirect throughout the night on enemy Roads and tracks in I2.B.C. and D. 4000 rounds were expended. The enemy aerial activity. Fairly quiet night.	A.A.G.

Army Form C. 2118.

WAR DIARY
or
INTELLIGENCE SUMMARY.

(Erase heading not required.)

Instructions regarding War Diaries and Intelligence Summaries are contained in F. S. Regs., Part II. and the Staff Manual respectively. Title pages will be prepared in manuscript.

Place	Date	Hour	Summary of Events and Information	Remarks and references to Appendices
GREEN-LAND HILL SECTOR	7		Our artillery fairly active on enemy's front line. 6.7's and howitzers. Enemy artillery not very active. But own support lines came in for a good deal of attention during the afternoon. Enemy Trench Mortars fairly active on front line with increased activity on support lines between 2.30pm and 2.50pm. Indirect fire was carried out by our Machine Gun during the night on enemy 6.1/2's and tracks. 2000 rounds being expended. An enemy aeroplane was brought down by our own planes and L.G. fire falling in enemy's lines behind WART TRENCH. Blue Clouds of smoke were observed rising from behind RAILWAY COPSE. during the day. Night fairly quiet.	J.J.
	8		A continual Bombardment was carried out by own artillery of the enemy's lines between 9am and 11am. From 2pm to 5pm a destructive shoot was carried out at 8.45 the Centre and R. Coy (Infantry)	J.J.

WAR DIARY
or
INTELLIGENCE SUMMARY

Army Form C. 2118.

Place	Date	Hour	Summary of Events and Information	Remarks and references to Appendices
GREEN-LAND HILL SECTOR.	8		acted for Artillery Counter Aggressiveness, and our artillery opened fire on "A" Switch with accurate and effective fire. Enemy artillery was fairly active on Support lines throughout the day. Night quiet. Harrassing M.G. fire was kept up in a normal in enemy's tracks and B.V. during the night; also in rear of Front line in suspected areas to prevent repairs by the enemy. 2000 rounds were expended. Enemy M.G. normal. Enemy observed sweeping parapets at intervals during the night. During the day Enemy Balloons were in position at 260°, 63°, 31°, 18° and 90° from H.II.a.95.35. (True Bearings): there were only up for a short time. The effect of our artillery shoot observed on WALNUT I.5.a. and very good. Direct hits observed on the foreman during the afternoon I.14.a.a.g.	M.L.
	9.		Our artillery fairly active during the forenoon. During the afternoon	Y.L.

Army Form C. 2118.

WAR DIARY
or
INTELLIGENCE SUMMARY.

(Erase heading not required.)

Instructions regarding War Diaries and Intelligence Summaries are contained in F. S. Regs., Part II. and the Staff Manual respectively. Title pages will be prepared in manuscript.

Place	Date	Hour	Summary of Events and Information	Remarks and references to Appendices
GREEN-LAND HILL SECTOR.	9		Shelling was confined chiefly to bursts - Battery Work. Little firing on both sides during the night. Our machine guns drenched and swept enemy tracks in I.2.d.1.3 and I.8.t. and I.9.a. during the night. 8000 rounds being expended. Enemy M.Gs. below normal. No aerial activity on either side.	J.G.
	10		Our artillery less active than usual. Enemy front and support lines were shelled intermittently during the day. C.T. also coming in for attention. Machine gun kept up a harassing fire on enemy tracks and C.T. throughout the night 6000 rounds being expended. Enemy Machine guns traversing C.T. and searching for ration parties during the night fired long bursts. During the night enemy appeared to have been working on trench at about I.9.a.5.9.	J.G.

Army Form C. 2118.

WAR DIARY
or
INTELLIGENCE SUMMARY.
(Erase heading not required.)

Instructions regarding War Diaries and Intelligence Summaries are contained in F. S. Regs., Part II. and the Staff Manual respectively. Title pages will be prepared in manuscript.

Place	Date	Hour	Summary of Events and Information	Remarks and references to Appendices
GREEN-LAND HILL SECTOR	11	—	Our artillery shelled enemy's front line and supports at 10.30 am. During the afternoon hostile salvos were put into SQUARE WOOD. Enemy artillery fairly active in support line during the day. Night fairly quiet. Our Machine Guns harassed and searched enemy's roads and tracks leading to T.M's from I.8.a.9.5. to I.2.6.5.2. with bursts of fire during the night. WEASEL trench and roads leading to WHIP X. Roads were also searched. Enemy trenches were also searched. Enemy M.G's during the night.	Y.G.
	12		Passed without incident. Nothing unusual to report. Neuve intermittent artillery bombardment by both sides during the day. Sniper fire as usual was carried out by our machine guns during the day & night. 5000 rounds being expended. Usual harassing by enemy M.G's during the night, otherwise quiet.	Y.G.

WAR DIARY
INTELLIGENCE SUMMARY.

(Erase heading not required.)

Army Form C. 2118.

Place	Date	Hour	Summary of Events and Information	Remarks and references to Appendices
GREEN- LAND HILL SECTOR	13		Enemy front line & supports were shelled with 4.5" and 6" at 10.0 am and again from 12 to 2 pm. Our 18 pounders bombarded some targets from 12 midnight to 2.30 am. At 10 pm salvos of Gas Shells were sent into Enemy Reserve Line. Our machine guns fired indirect during the night searching HART ANWOOL and harassing NIBBLE AND HAYX. 6000 rounds were expended. A few of our planes were up during the day patrolling the front and were shelled by enemy A.A. Guns. Enemy machine guns very active during the night. Bombing and harassing. At 11.30 pm forms were heard in Enemy lines. Horns continued to be sounded during the night although there was no shelling.	M.S.
	14.		Our artillery fairly quiet during the morning. At intervals 1.15 - 2 pm. Our 18 pdrs fired 12 rounds every 10 minutes. At 5 pm our Heavies shelled enemy front	Y.S.

Army Form C. 2118.

WAR DIARY
or
INTELLIGENCE SUMMARY.

(Erase heading not required.)

Instructions regarding War Diaries and Intelligence Summaries are contained in F. S. Regs., Part II. and the Staff Manual respectively. Title pages will be prepared in manuscript.

Place	Date	Hour	Summary of Events and Information	Remarks and references to Appendices
GREENLAND HILL SECTOR.	14		Line opposite Left Front. Between 10-12 pm a few rounds were sent over at long intervals. Our Machine Guns fired indirect throughout the night engaging New trench I.8.a.7.1. to I.8.a. 85.95. and traversed W188zE AND N4V. 10,000 rounds were expended. Aerial activity inactive in both sides. Enemy Machine Guns very active sweeping parapet in the evening and early morning. The day passed without any unusual incidents.	Y.Y.
	15		Usual artillery activity on both sides but owing to poor visability no big shoots were carried out. During the afternoon our artillery registered for road in the RightRde. Sector Fire was opened at 6.30 pm the enemys support lines being bombarded. Our Machine Guns co-operated with above, firing on I.2.0.5.1. to I.8.a.5.4., and I.2.0.98.20. to I5.B.1.5. also on road from I2.0.59. to I.2.a.5.8. 43,000 rounds were expended. Enemy Machine Guns very active during operation harassing support	F.J.L

WAR DIARY
or
INTELLIGENCE SUMMARY.

(Erase heading not required.)

Army Form C. 2118.

Place	Date	Hour	Summary of Events and Information	Remarks and references to Appendices
GREEN-LANE HILL SECTOR	15		Trench and Communication trenches. Remainder of night quiet.	J.G.
	16.		Our artillery was very active during the morning shelling the enemy front and support lines. At 1pm heavy salvos were sent into enemy lines. From 6.30pm to 1? Midnight salvos were fired at intervals on to Enemy's Reserve lines and tracks. Enemy Artillery slightly increased. Our Machine Guns fired indirect throughout the night towards enemy WIBBLE and WAVY. 4000 rounds were expended. Enemy Machine guns active during night, traversing support lines and Communication Trenches. Visibility during day bad. Otherwise quiet.	J.G.
	17		Our artillery very active during the morning at 10.30 am Field Guns and howers bombarded enemy front and support lines. Activity slightly increased during the afternoon. Night fairly quiet.	J.G.

WAR DIARY
or
INTELLIGENCE SUMMARY.

(Erase heading not required.)

Army Form C. 2118.

Place	Date	Hour	Summary of Events and Information	Remarks and references to Appendices
GREEN-LANA HILL SECTOR	17		Enemy Artillery below normal. Our Machine Gun fired indirect throughout the night, engaging I.2.a.5.8. to I.2.c.95.80. 8000 rounds were expended. Enemy Machine Gun very active throughout the night with occasional long bursts on our lines. Aerial activity on both sides normal. Nothing incidental throughout the day to report.	J.G.
	18		Our successful raid was carried out from 3.0 pm to 3.10 pm with which our Machine Gun co-operated 20,000 rounds being expended. During the smoke discharge a party of the enemy attempted to cross to our lines but were dispersed by our M.G's L.G's and rifle fire. Enemy Machine Guns were very active during our smoke discharge. Aerial activity on both sides normal. In retaliation to Smoke attack Enemy Artillery heavily bombarded our front and support lines. Our Artillery was very active throughout front and support — the day shelling enemy's front and support lines.	J.G.

Army Form C. 2118.

WAR DIARY
or
INTELLIGENCE SUMMARY.
(Erase heading not required.)

Instructions regarding War Diaries and Intelligence
Summaries are contained in F. S. Regs., Part II.
and the Staff Manual respectively. Title pages
will be prepared in manuscript.

Place	Date	Hour	Summary of Events and Information	Remarks and references to Appendices
GREEN-LAND HILL SECTOR	19	—	A successful raid was carried out by the 2/7 R. Sussex on enemy trenches, a number of the enemy were killed and 1 prisoner belonging to the 457 Inf. captured. Our artillery back very active shelling enemys front and support lines. Enemy Artillery below normal. Our machine guns fired in co-operation with above raid. 35,000 rounds being expended. Artillery activity normal. Night quiet	A.J.G.
	20	—	Our artillery kept up a harassing fire throughout the day on enemy front and support trenches. About 8 p.m. violent fire was opened on to enemy line lasting about 5 minutes, there was no retaliation. Enemy Artillery much below normal our front and support were lightly shelled at big intervals throughout the day. Our Machine guns fired indirect during the night. 4000 rounds being expended.	A.J.G.

WAR DIARY
or
INTELLIGENCE SUMMARY

Army Form C. 2118.

(Erase heading not required.)

Place	Date	Hour	Summary of Events and Information	Remarks and references to Appendices
GREENLAND HILL SECTOR	21		The Company was relieved by 163 Machine Gun Company, relief was complete by 12.30 pm, and section marched independently to ARRAS.	
ARRAS	22		The Company cleaned guns, equipment and uniforms.	
	23		Company training	
	24		Company training	
	25		Company training and Bath	
	26		Inspection of Transport by Brig-Genl. Lumsdg. 182 Infty Bde. and Company training	
	27		Company training.	
	28		Company moved to Dainville arriving in billets by 12.45pm	
DAINVILLE	29		Company training.	
DAINVILLE	30		Company less Transport entrained at BEAUMETZ for BAPAUME detraining at 11am. after waiting for about 2 hours at BAPAUME	
BAPAUME			the Company was embussed and embussing at RUYAULCOURT and	
TRESCAULT			marched to TRESCAULT where the Company rested for the night under Canvas.	

A.W. Mitchell
for O.C. 182 M.G. Coy.

204"

Nº 185 Machine Gun Coy

War Diary

From 1st December 1917 to 31st December 1917

(Volume XIX)

Confidential

WAR DIARY
INTELLIGENCE SUMMARY

182 M.G. Coy

VOLUME XIX

Place	Date	Hour	Summary of Events and Information	Remarks and references to Appendices
HAVRIN-COURT WOOD	1.		Orders received at 4 am to proceed to HEUDECOURT where the Brigade was massing. Company reached HEUDECOURT about 10 am where further instructions were awaited. No instructions to move were received, the Company bivouacing for the night.	
GOUZEAU-COURT WOOD	2		at 10 am under instructions from Brigade Headqrs the Company marched to GOUZEAUCOURT WOOD arriving about 10 am. During this period the wood was heavily shelled at 5 pm the Company moved into the line in relief of 61st Machine Gun Company N. of LA VACQUERIE. The 61st Machine Gun Company had only 3 guns left with 15 men. Reference 57.c.S.E. (2). Line taken up and held with 12 guns running roughly from R.3.b.9.2. to R.9.d.5.9. Four guns in support of original Hindenburg front line in R.3.c and R.9.a	
N of LA VACQUERIE	3		Gun positions unchanged. Heavy enemy shelling along	

WAR DIARY
or
INTELLIGENCE SUMMARY.

(Erase heading not required.)

Army Form C. 2118.

Place	Date	Hour	Summary of Events and Information	Remarks and references to Appendices
N. of LA VACQUERIE	3		The whole Brigade Front and Support lines LA VACQUERIE in strength during the day and captured the village. Enemy attacked Night fairly quiet. Position unchanged	A.G.
	4		Enemy again attacked on the front of Brigade on our right and forced them to give a little ground, this necessitated four Reserve Guns being brought into position on line running from R.9.d.5.9. to N.6 B.1.9. Casualties during period very slight. Heavy shelling along whole Brigade Area	A.G.
	5	6 am	5th Decr. very slight. Ration and water supply during the period worked well. Communication supply more difficult on account of number of men away from the Company and the impossibility of getting Carrying parties from the Infantry. Position unchanged Heavy shelling by the Enemy on astd Brigade front. during day and intermittent	

WAR DIARY
or
INTELLIGENCE SUMMARY.

Army Form C. 2118.

Place	Date	Hour	Summary of Events and Information	Remarks and references to Appendices
N. of LA VACQUERIE	5		Shelling during night. A certain amount of Field Artillery used by the ~~Battery~~ enemy was British.	J.G.
	6th		Artillery activity much lighter. Enemy Barrage on French and Gun trailers running from R.9.a.5.9. to R.15.b.1.9 for ½ an hour about midday. 1 Gun was put out of action. Company relieved by 109 Machine Gun Company during the night.	J.G.
HAPLIN- COURT WOOD	7th		Company minus 6 guns on Barrage duties in rear of HAPLINCOURT WOOD.	J.G.
	8		Company in rest. Bivouacs heavily shelled by enemy 4.2" and bombed by enemy planes. This necessitated moving in Bivouacs to another part of the wood. 3 casualties sustained and 1 Reading horse slightly injured.	J.G.

Army Form C. 2118.

WAR DIARY
or
INTELLIGENCE SUMMARY.
(Erase heading not required.)

Place	Date	Hour	Summary of Events and Information	Remarks and references to Appendices
HAYRIN-COURT WOOD	9		Company paraded at 10.0 a.m. for G.O.C. division. Day quiet. Company moved into the line as if relieved 14th Machine Gun Coy. in line N. of LA VACQUERIE	✓
W. of LA VACQUERIE	10.		Relief carried out with only 1 casualty. Seven guns placed in forward position. 8 guns in Barrage Battery. Intermittent shelling during day and night.	✓ G.S.
	11		Position unchanged. Enemy aircraft very active. Our artillery replied heavily to hostile artillery activity.	✓ G.S.
	12		Our artillery very active. M.G. positions unchanged. 1 gun in forward area knocked out by shell fire, who was replaced immediately. Night quiet.	✓ G.S.
	13		Enemy artillery unusually quiet. Our artillery active. Enemy planes over our lines during greater part of day at low altitude. 1 Enemy Observation Balloon brought down by our planes.	✓ G.S.
	14.		Prisoner captured stated that enemy would attack this morning along whole Divisional front at 6.20 a.m. Our artillery	✓ G.S.

WAR DIARY
or
INTELLIGENCE SUMMARY.

(Erase heading not required.)

Army Form C. 2118.

Place	Date	Hour	Summary of Events and Information	Remarks and references to Appendices
W. of LA VACQUERIE	14		and Machine Gun Barraged all enemy approaches. Attack did not take place. Enemy Artillery still unusually quiet.	J.J.
	15		Position unchanged. Enemy artillery not active on our back areas. Enemy planes also flying over our lines in large numbers. Machine Gun Barrage Battery opened with our artillery in above shoot during day and night.	J.J.
	16		Seven forward positions and guns from Barrage Battery relieved by 184 Machine Gun Company. These Gun teams withdrew to Bivouacs in HAYRINCOURT WOOD. Remaining 6 guns in Barrage position under O.C. 184 Machine Gun Company. Relief completed by 10.30am	J.J.
HAYRIN-COURT WOOD	17		Company in Rest.	J.C.
	18		Company minus personnel in Barrage position moved to Billets in MANANCOURT arriving at 4 pm.	J.C.

WAR DIARY
or
INTELLIGENCE SUMMARY.
(Erase heading not required.)

Army Form C. 2118.

Place	Date	Hour	Summary of Events and Information	Remarks and references to Appendices
MARAN-COURT	19	—	Company training	
	20		Company training. 6 Guns in Brigade trials under O.B. 184 Machine Gun Company will be under instructions from Divisional Headquarters.	
	21		Arrived at MARANCOURT arriving at 10.30 a.m. Company training	O.C.
	22		Company training	O.C.
	23		Company entrained at CORBIE at 9.0 am (two companies) detrained at CORBIE at 2.0 pm marched to Billets in SAILLY-LE-SEC arriving about 4.0 pm.	O.C.
SAILLY-LE-SEC.	24		Transport from V Corps to XVIII Corps sent by hand. Bde transferred from V Corps to XVIII Corps.	O.C.
	25		Company transport arrived about 2.0 pm. (Company rested. Christmas day)	O.C.
	26		Company rested.	O.C.
	27		Company training	O.C.
	28		Company training and Inspection by Bde Commander	O.C.

Army Form C. 2118.

WAR DIARY
or
INTELLIGENCE SUMMARY.
(Erase heading not required.)

Instructions regarding War Diaries and Intelligence Summaries are contained in F. S. Regs., Part II. and the Staff Manual respectively. Title pages will be prepared in manuscript.

Place	Date	Hour	Summary of Events and Information	Remarks and references to Appendices
SAILLY-LE-SEC.	29	-	Company training	
AUBERCOURT	30	-	Company marched to AUBERCOURT	
	31	-	Company marched to FRESNOY-EN-CHAUSSEE	

J. G. Cooke. Major
Commanding 182 Machine Gun Coy

WAR DIARY
or
INTELLIGENCE SUMMARY.
(Erase heading not required.)

Army Form C. 2118.

182 M Guy Coy

Volume XX

Place	Date	Hour	Summary of Events and Information	Remarks and references to Appendices
FRESNOY-EN-CHAUSSEE	1	-	Company Training	
	2	-	Company Training	
	3	-	Company Training	
	4	-	Company Training	
	5	-	Company Training	
	6	-	Company Training. Looking limbers for moving to move Baths.	
BILLANCOURT	7		Company moved to BILLANCOURT under 2nd in command O.C. Company with Lieuts. COLLEN and DOUGLAS and Brigade Major Lt HESLE and succeeded by Lieuts. COLBY to VERMAND and accommodated about SW of ST QUENTIN ACR 1474 FRENCH REGT.	
"	8.		Company at BILLANCOURT inspection of recent journeying. Major Levy Commanding 2nd Army visited SHQ 11-10-20 mm. at which OC Lieuts of Brigade were present.	

Instructions regarding War Diaries and Intelligence Summaries are contained in F. S. Regs., Part II. and the Staff Manual respectively. Title pages will be prepared in manuscript.

Army Form C. 2118.

WAR DIARY
or
INTELLIGENCE SUMMARY.
(Erase heading not required.)

Instructions regarding War Diaries and Intelligence Summaries are contained in F. S. Regs., Part II. and the Staff Manual respectively. Title pages will be prepared in manuscript.

Place	Date	Hour	Summary of Events and Information	Remarks and references to Appendices
SAVY	9		Battalion marched to SAVY from BILLANCOURT — route MAGAZINE — MATIGNY — DOUILLY — FOREST — GERMAINE — VEAUX — ETREILLERS — SAVY	
SAVY	10		O.C. Coy. with Lieuts. Cullen Dugger & Greer proceeded up the line. Arrangements made by M.G.O. 74th French Regt. made for going into line	
S.Iv.C.30.g.i Ref S.620 SW 1.30,000	11		Battalion proceeded into line. Enemy Savy at 8 a.m. Chief reports complete by 11 a.m. No 4 Section on left at FAYET. No 1 Section in middle Big Wood. No 3 Section Bois du Rozet. No 2 Section in right in front of FRANCILLY SELENCY. No 2 Section inverse with line found at position about 200 yds long COTTAGES M. SELENCY. FAYET R.I. and two guns in front of CROWS QUARRY.	
do.	12		Hostile activity of Enemy Artillery fairly active, at following points, vicinity of BOIS DES AMBOISES, DEE COPSE, OLD MILL FAYET, MAISSEMY, HOLNON Rd. Rounds 105th found on MAISSAIX WORK, RED Flag found. 50L. FM. Hostile M.G. fire for over during Quentin QUENTIN FAYET and ST SAVY. ST QUENTIN Rd.	

Army Form C. 2118.

WAR DIARY
or
INTELLIGENCE SUMMARY.
(Erase heading not required.)

Instructions regarding War Diaries and Intelligence Summaries are contained in F. S. Regs., Part II. and the Staff Manual respectively. Title pages will be prepared in manuscript.

Place	Date	Hour	Summary of Events and Information	Remarks and references to Appendices
Field c 30 9a	13		(D OVR OSIRI	
			Distribution of reinforcements during enemy	
			Enemy attacked but were beaten to ENUYL about his defences E of GSPY FM.	
			Enemy left a force observing trench in early morning but was driven	
			S17b.66 five who were but the enemy later in day sent further patrols	
			Artillery. active in STUYBAS - HOLNON - FAYET and SOMENCY ridges.	
			HOLNON – FAYET Rd. and SOMENCY HOLNON Rd. Shell nearly 77mm bearing on	
			M.G. intermittent fire during O.P. N- W of old county Rd and SEQUEHART Rd	
			Sent battery enemy planes helpful	J.C
			West of Z fos. Suspected of being engaged in camp movements of	
			Aviation	
	14		Weather. Artillery. actively intelligent. Registration continued west	
			of xxx n.u. D.G. Enemy planes engaged throughout by infantry	
			Scout Aeroplanes very active over Enemy lines	
			Enemy. Artillery. Desultory throughout day. No known targets	
			Inf. Occasional bursts during the day to serve as alarms	
			forces P. Enemy of track... ...during the day in the line	J.C

WAR DIARY
or
INTELLIGENCE SUMMARY.
(Erase heading not required.)

Army Form C. 2118.

Place	Date	Hour	Summary of Events and Information	Remarks and references to Appendices
CG.	15.		Operations	
			General. Artillery very quiet - being too misty to our Artillery & hostile counter batteries	
			M.G. S.A. occasional bursts by hostile M.Gs during night	
			Patrols. Reported by Army very little of importance	
			2. Enemy. Artillery Very Quiet. Hostile field Howitzers fired in QUARRY	
			M.G. Hostile M.Gs fired occasionally in FAYET & OLD ROMAN RD	
			Evening. Hostile M.Gs fired occasionally on approach to our front line	J.16
	16.		1. Operations Artillery Quiet but during Restaurant	
			Infantry Patrols carried out, from Battalions	
			M.G. Nil	
			2. Enemy Artillery Slow Domined activity during evening FAYET R? & FAYET	
			M.G. Usual harassing fire during night.	
			4.4K Dom. General. Enemy employed considerably large increased working and carrying	J.16
			in vicinity	

WAR DIARY
or
INTELLIGENCE SUMMARY.
(Erase heading not required.)

Army Form C. 2118.

Place	Date	Hour	Summary of Events and Information	Remarks and references to Appendices
	17.		Relief of Battalion. ARTILLERY. Few rounds on Coy HQrs. Quiet. Shrapnel over ours.	
			MESSINES & N.E.C. front into we held by our battalion.	
			M/g. P.E. Quiet. Except Lys front from hrs.	
			T.M. few rounds fired on Coy HQs.	
			Weather. Cloudy & turning bucky. Aeroplane recon by	
	18.		Enemy. Artillery Activity during afternoon	
			Our Arm. Rtnd at S.O.S & reported front line on	
			S. & b. C.	
			Successfully front line and reserves Coy HQs.	
			MG. nil	
			Company relieved by 182 M.G.C. relief broken compltly by 11 p.m.	
			Section on relief marched independently to VAUX.	

WAR DIARY
or
INTELLIGENCE SUMMARY.

Army Form C. 2118.

Place	Date	Hour	Summary of Events and Information	Remarks and references to Appendices
VAUX	19.		Company training PT. Inspections & deficiency return etc	
	20.		Company training PT Church Parade	
	21.		Company Training P.T. S.D. Close order Drill Saluting	
	22.		Company morning. Platoon gun drill. Close order drill. Inspections etc	
	23.		Company training PT. R.G.D. Close order drill. Lewis gun drill	
	24.		Company training PT. Tactical exercise. Close order drill. Lewis gun drill	
	25.		Company training PT. Command drill. Close order drill. Sect Apprch drill. N.C.O. and Section Officers proceeded up the line to reconnoitre left sector and arrange relief of 11th M.G.C.	
	26.		My instructions for going into the line. Company relieved 124 M.G. in Left Sector. relief reported complete to Bn Hq. Keep 2d-Houdain 9.30 P.M.	
TAESNEY	27.		12 Guns in forward area & in reserve. Day & night exceedingly quiet. Enemy machine gun harassing fire throughout the	
LE PETIT			night. Our own guns fired gas shell & fire to keep same in working order	

WAR DIARY
or
INTELLIGENCE SUMMARY.
(Erase heading not required.)

Army Form C. 2118.

Place	Date	Hour	Summary of Events and Information	Remarks and references to Appendices
FRESNOY LE PETIT	28		Day quite very quiet — reported by Coyd on L 3 Battn the hostile side. Usual activity on both sides. Several our own planes flying at day break — shower rain fog 3. no firing close enough for our A.A. + few bursts 8-6 feet up	
-do-	29		Position unchanged. Very little artillery activity — all quiet + snowing. Actual activity rest. Lewaster had a great deal of low flying. Passed out by M.G. machine.	JRC
-do-	30		Position unchanged. Slight snow at day activity particularly on FRESNOY LE PETIT + PONTRUET. our own [?] also — great aerial activity on our side — great [?] by enemy planes up during the morning — fell over with heavy AA fire from battery + H.Q.	JRC

Army Form C. 2118.

WAR DIARY
or
INTELLIGENCE SUMMARY.
(Erase heading not required.)

Instructions regarding War Diaries and Intelligence Summaries are contained in F. S. Regs., Part II. and the Staff Manual respectively. Title pages will be prepared in manuscript.

Place	Date	Hour	Summary of Events and Information	Remarks and references to Appendices
FRESNOY LE PETIT	31		Positions unchanged. Khun a list which mainly told - ours artillery fire in either side is rested activity. No M.G. fire. Enemy M.G.'s active during night with harassing fire.	App

J.C. Cook Major
Cmdg N° 182 M.G. Coy

61 Bn M.G. Corps.
I

182 Machine Gun Company.

War Diary

From February 1st to February 28th

(Volume 21)

WAR DIARY or INTELLIGENCE SUMMARY.

(Erase heading not required.)

Army Form C. 2118.

(Volume 2)

Place	Date	Hour	Summary of Events and Information	Remarks and references to Appendices
FRESNOY LE PETIT	1st		Positions unchanged. No artillery activity on either side. Weather dull & misty.	App. 2
	2nd		Aeroplane clear - good aerial activity on both sides - no E.A. brought down. Enemy artillery busy registering during p.m. No shooting - no artillery during the afternoon.	App.
	3rd		Little artillery activity. Aircraft busy - enemy machines frequently coming in line at a great altitude. Registering by artillery on both sides. Several hundred rounds fired by our M.G's on enemy planes. Enemy M.G. fire at frequent intervals during night.	App.
	4th		No artillery activity on either side. Atmosphere thick & cloudy. No aerial activity. Enemy M.G. active during night with harassing fire in FRESNOY & BRICOURT.	App.
	5th		Renewed aerial activity. Artillery on both sides very quiet. Our planes passed low over our lines at 6.30 P.M. apparently on bombing expedition.	App.

WAR DIARY
or
INTELLIGENCE SUMMARY.

(Erase heading not required.)

Army Form C. 2118.

Place	Date	Hour	Summary of Events and Information	Remarks and references to Appendices
FRESNOY LE PETIT.	6th		Enemy artillery were active from Woolah in cemetery at FRESNOY LE PETIT. He appeared to be registering on his front-line batteries & M.M's & M.G's. No enemy aerial activity — our planes up during afternoon. A few rounds fired by us to L.T. guns.	J.C.
"	7th		Wet & dull during day. Very little artillery on either side.	J.C.
	8th		Activity on either side. No round of fired by M.G.s. Enemy Artillery registered during morning on various points along our line during afternoon. Our guns were registering. Few planes up during the whole day. 6 enemy machines attempted to cross our line at 4.30 PM but were driven off by A.A fire.	J.C.
	9th		Still but observation good — slight increase artillery activity on both sides — a few of our planes up — no enemy planes seen. — No firing done by M.G. except few M.G's.	J.C.
	10th		Enemy Artillery active during the day. PONTRUET receiving much attention. The cemetery at FRESNOY also came in for slight shelling. Our own artillery active.	J.C.

WAR DIARY
or
INTELLIGENCE SUMMARY.
(Erase heading not required.)

Army Form C. 2118.

Place	Date	Hour	Summary of Events and Information	Remarks and references to Appendices
FRESNOY LE PETIT	10		Enemy sent up flare at intervals during the day with Standers. Melted. Aerial activity on both sides normal. Enemy plans who attempted to cross our lines were heavily shelled by our AA guns. Night quiet.	
	11		Enemy activity with artillery rather above normal. Our front, support line and back area were heavily shelled during the day, and no mean the cemetery at FRESNOY came in for a good deal of shelling. Aerial activity below normal. The Company was relieved by 183 Machine Gun Company and relief on file by 9 p.m. On completion Company proceeded to Billets at VAUX. 2 gun teams on AA duty	Joe
VAUX	12		at BEAUVOIS. Company training	Joe
	13		Company training	Joe

WAR DIARY
or
INTELLIGENCE SUMMARY.

Army Form C. 2118.

Place	Date	Hour	Summary of Events and Information	Remarks and references to Appendices
VAUX	14		Company Training. Section Officers Lecture. Sergt's & No. 1. Reconnoitred Gun positions in reserve Battle Zone.	J/C
	15	-	Company Training	do
	16	-	Company Training	do
	17	-	Company Training. Major J.O. COOK (B.O.) to Senior Officers Conference XVIII Corps. H'dqrs.	do
	18	-	Company Training and preparation for line	do
	19	-	Company moved into line. Right Sector in relief of 164 Machine Gun Company, leaving VAUX at 4.0 p.m. relief complete by 9.0 p.m. On completion of relief disposition of Company as follows:- Company Headquarters S.10.e.35.9. Mr FRANCILLY-SILENCY. No 1 Section FAYET. No 2 Section BOIS DE ROSES. No 4 Section MANCHESTER HILL. No 3 Section Mobile Guns. Artillery on both sides quiet. Visibility poor.	J/C

S.10.e.35.9.0

WAR DIARY
or
INTELLIGENCE SUMMARY.
(Erase heading not required.)

Army Form C. 2118.

Place	Date	Hour	Summary of Events and Information	Remarks and references to Appendices
S.10 c 35 9	20	—	Slight aerial activity on both sides otherwise quiet.	A 36
	21	"	Slightly fair. Enemy Artillery fairly active on Back Areas FAYET receiving much attention.	
			Aerial activity on both sides above normal. Several enemy planes crossed our lines during the day but were driven back by A.A. fire. Several of our planes between 6 and 7 on crossed the enemy lines on a bombing expedition. Machine guns in both sides normal.	
	22.		Weather fair. Our artillery fired at intervals on enemy trenches and reserve system. Enemy retaliation was normal. Aerial activity on both sides below normal. No account of welfare weather.	Ad
	23		about 9.30 p.m. our 18 pounders shelled the enemy front line opposite FAYET. The right of ST QUENTIN was lightly shelled between 10 and 2 p.m. at 8.55 p.m.	for

WAR DIARY
or
INTELLIGENCE SUMMARY.
(Erase heading not required.)

Army Form C. 2118.

Place	Date	Hour	Summary of Events and Information	Remarks and references to Appendices
S.10.0.35.9	23		enemy Artillery opened fire all along our front and continued shelling until 9.20 p.m. FAYET receiving much attention 4.2" and 77 m.m. In retaliation to this Bombardment our Howitzers opened fire from 9 p.m. to 9.20 p.m. on enemy front line opposite our Div. Front. At 1 p.m. M.G.'s at (S.10.b.75.35) fired 750 rounds on to S.O.S. lines or S.O.S. signal being sent up. Aerial activity normal. Both sides patrolling during the day. Guns in the following factions were relieved by G.S. Machine Gun Company. Relief completed by 11.0 p.m. No. 1 Co. No. 15, 17, 18, 19, 33, 34, 35, 36. Relief guns withdrew to the following new position:- 1 Gun to ENGHEIN Redoubt and M.33.D.8.2. Two guns to S.3.d.95.75 and S.3.d.5.7. one gun to S.9.c.9a. 2 guns to S.10.a.45.50. and S.10.a.70.25. No. 3 gun	

WAR DIARY
or
INTELLIGENCE SUMMARY.

Army Form C. 2118.

Place	Date	Hour	Summary of Events and Information	Remarks and references to Appendices
S.10.c.35.9.	23		Moved to N.E. corner of BOIS de ROSES. (S.11.a.05.05) (all map References Ref. map 62. B.S.W.)	
	24		Our artillery showed an increased activity. Enemy trench mortars and OERY FARM and FAUBOURG ST JEAN were shelled. Slight increase in enemy artillery activity. SQUASH VALLEY and S.4.d (vicinity of ENGHIEN REDOUBT) were shelled with 105mm shells. Occasional shelling of OREN with 105mm shells.	
			S.5.c. and FAYET with 105mm during the day. Our lines were shelled practically the whole of the day 7-10.10pm a bombing squadron flew over our lines. Not much wire activity worked during day. Night fairly quiet. Night fairly quiet.	
	25		Artillery activity slight on both sides. Our 18 pounders shelled the enemy's new system lightly during the day. FAYET was lightly shelled by the	

WAR DIARY
or
INTELLIGENCE SUMMARY.
(Erase heading not required.)

Army Form C. 2118.

Place	Date	Hour	Summary of Events and Information	Remarks and references to Appendices
S.10.c.35.9.	25		Enemy during the day at 9.30 am. commenced a bit raid on our left by Lord STRATHCONAS HORSE. Our artillery carried out a bombardment of the enemy front system opposite FAYET which lasted 15 minutes. Retaliation by the enemy slight. Bombardment on slight. Nº 267 machine Gun Company both gave the following Festubert fire 182. M.G. Coy H.35.d.2.3. H.33.c.H8.65 and H.33.d.80.10 (3guns) 4 guns then withdrew to the following positions X.11.a. 50.90 and X.17.B.90.20. (Battle zone position.)	
	26		Our artillery was very active registration with aerial observation being carried out. FAUBOURG ST JEAN and area T.13.B. were shelled with heavies. Our aircraft were very active constantly flying over enemy's lines, they were heavily engaged with anti aircraft and machine gun fire.	

WAR DIARY
or
INTELLIGENCE SUMMARY.

Army Form C. 2118.

Place	Date	Hour	Summary of Events and Information	Remarks and references to Appendices
S.10.c.35.9	26	-	of DOUGLAS COPSE were shelled with 77mm between 9.20 and 10.30am. About noon a few light shells fell in ENGHIEN Redoubt. Between 4.50 and 5.20pm enemy fired 12. 105 MM on THREE COTTAGES, FAYET and also shelled with 105MM during this period. Our Machine Guns normal. Enemy Machine Guns very active against our planes during the day. During the night usual bursts and throwing flare. Enemy Aeroplanes very active were not always with us. A.A. and Machine Gun fire. Night normal S.O.C.	
	27		Artillery activity of both sides. Slight. Our artillery shelled the enemy front system in front of ST QUENTIN with 18 pounders at intervals during the day. THREE COTTAGES, SQUASH VALLEY and vicinity of FAYET were lightly shelled at intervals during the day. Our machine Guns fired at enemy aircraft	

WAR DIARY
or
INTELLIGENCE SUMMARY.
(Erase heading not required.)

Army Form C. 2118.

Instructions regarding War Diaries and Intelligence Summaries are contained in F. S. Regs., Part II. and the Staff Manual respectively. Title pages will be prepared in manuscript.

Place	Date	Hour	Summary of Events and Information	Remarks and references to Appendices
S.10.c.35.9.	27	27.	During the day Enemy aerial activity during the afternoon. From 2.35 pm until 3.0 pm two hostile planes were flying low over our lines. They were heavily engaged with M.G fire. At 3.0 pm two E.A attempted to cross our lines but on the observance of two of our scouts they made off towards their own lines. 9/6 Warwicks relieved 9/6 Worcesters in the forward zone. Night quiet.	
	28	28.	Artillery activity on or back areas did not show much activity. Enemy Back Areas were lightly shelled by our 18 pounders during the afternoon. Enemy shelled F4 E7 during the day with H.2.5. No unusual aerial activity on either side. Machine Guns normal. Night quiet.	J.O.C

Major
Commanding N°. 62 Machine Gun Bn.

www.ingramcontent.com/pod-product-compliance
Lightning Source LLC
Chambersburg PA
CBHW081422160426

43193CB00013B/2172